The Irreverent Guide to Spectacular Communication

Take Charge
of Your Words
and Craft a
Greater Life

LB Adams

Mention of specific companies, organizations, authorities or individuals in this book does not imply endorsement by the author or publisher, nor does mention of specific companies, organizations, authorities or individuals imply that they endorse this book, its author or the publisher.

Internet addresses referenced in this book were accurate at the time it went to press.

©2021 by LB Adams

Book design by Andrew Barton
www.andrewbartondesign.com

ISBN-978-1-7372193-0-9 Paperback
ISBN-978-1-7372193-1-6 Ebook
ISBN-978-1-7372193-2-3 Audio

For the women who led me — June, Elizabeth & Gabriella

For the women who walk beside me — Janet, Tanya, Diana, Angela, Pamala & Gab

and David

Table of Contents

Introduction

Scene 1

Theatre saved my life.

Literally, saved my life.

I grew up poor in Upstate New York to parents who, given the extreme trauma that they each endured as children, probably should never have had children of their own.

Decent grades and financial aid allowed me to run away to college in New York City. Going to college was something that my parents didn't necessarily agree with, but didn't have the fortitude to prohibit. They knew I was "different" and needed to get out.

As a child, I was always writing stories and putting on dance parties, and making costumes and getting my sisters to participate in my "dramatics." I've been reading since I was four years old. Words are everything to me.

In the 7th grade, when I made my decision to not join the Air Force and to not become a hairstylist, there was only one path I could imagine — that of an actor. Becoming an actor meant that I would learn how not to be afraid.

When you grow up with people who terrify you, the idea of being fearless is, well...spectacular.

I wanted to live on the stage, adored and applauded by everyone. Life hasn't worked out exactly that way, but my love of the theatre, and of the ways we humans interact with each other, hasn't changed at all. Through many jobs and career changes, I've kept and held, and most importantly, used, all of the great lessons the theatre had to give me.

The ways and whys of human communication is endlessly fascinating, ridiculous and sometimes stupendously funny to me. We almost never say what we actually mean, and when we do, we muck it up with poor word choices or inconsistent body language. Our scripts are packed with text, sub-text and sub-sub-sub text. We're a tangled mess of communication contradictions.

We can do better. We can be spectacular.

As my Dad said when he and my Mom dropped me off in New York City a month before my 18th birthday, "Here's $20 bucks, go learn stuff."

Perhaps we can learn stuff together.

2

Introduction

Scene 2

This book is probably not for you if...

You're the kind of person who easily glides in and out of conversations during a networking event. If you have never felt a bit of stark fear when speaking in front of others. Or if you've managed to reach a certain age without the words "social anxiety" entering your personal vocabulary. If any of these apply to you, this book is definitely not for you. So go on. Move along, nothing to see here.

If, however...

You find that social interaction takes thoughtfulness, if you believe public speaking is something that you want to be able to do without puking on your shoes, or if you understand that empathy might be a skill (and not a weakness!), then you're reading the right book.

This book is not for the polished or perfect. It's not for firmly entrenched conglomerate CEOs basking in their top 1%-ness. Nor is it for anyone looking for "tricks" or "life hacks." I don't work that way.

Rather, it is for anyone looking to put authentic effort into growing their interpersonal skills. This book might be right for you if you're looking to step up. To level-up your skills — and to look at the world, the way we move through it, and the conversations that drive us — a bit differently.

This is a business book — a professional development guidebook of sorts designed to give the reader real insight and a view of how to move through your professional interactions with more intention and awareness. I wrote it with women in mind, yet nothing in these pages is exclusive to women. It's also a personal growth tour. In these pages, you'll find: a smörgåsbord of information on small ways to level-up, expert opinions, a little snarky humor, and more than a couple of curse words. You'll also find solid skill-building knowledge on a wide variety of soft skills — along with stories of real people implementing those skills.

The professional development/personal growth field is staggeringly wide and deep. I encourage you to do as I have done and learn from as many people as you can — in as many ways as you can. To that end, at the end of this book you'll find a variety of people and resources to supplement your learning journey.

Back to the script at hand…

This book is built for professionals — the people who work with other people. Because let's face it — people are difficult. They rarely do what you want them to do, or think they should do. They almost never say what they mean, and they have the absolute gall to have thoughts and opinions and points of views that are radically different from your own. There is SO MUCH data out there that talks about the value of soft skills — both ideally and empirically — which you'll see a lot of in this book.

Let's *also* not forget logic. It makes good common sense to learn how to interact well with people in a variety of circumstances using a variety of skills. It just does.

If you're someone who is simply *unsatisfied* with where you find yourself on the road of life, we've got tips and walk-out-the-door ideas to help you move your needle.

Regardless if you're fresh out of college, deep into your fourth career, or somewhere else on your journey, this book will make you more employable, help you earn more money, and provide you with a greater understanding of your daily interactions with other humans.

At the end of the day, this book IS FOR YOU if you want information, guidance and actionable ways to grow your own skills or the skills of people you manage or team with.

If after all of this, you're still here — congratulations! This book is indeed for you.

In the coming chapters, I'll break down a variety of soft skills into bite-sized concepts and awarenesses. No skill is built, grown, or evolved without first understanding where you are *now*. So get prepared to look honestly at where you are currently, where you'd like to be, what you think you lack, and where your awesomeness lies.

This book uses **theatre strategies** as the basis of everything. That doesn't mean that I'll demand that you learn Hamlet's "To be or not to be…" monologue.

Unless you want to, but hey, that's on you.

What I mean is that soft skills are human skills, and actors and performers have a unique view into human communication and interaction. It means that to grow, you must do. It also provides us with a really cool perspective for observation and education.

It means that in a creative studio, we always ask two questions:

1. What worked and is worth repeating?

2. What needs improvement?

Imagine the difficult scenario of asking your boss for a raise. You rehearse the conversation, noting the value you bring to the company, and the reasons it is appropriate for them to throw money at you. The big moment arrives and you are able to calmly and plainly state your case, even though you've completely forgotten your boss's name. You get the dollars, but it's not as much as you'd like.

Ask yourself:

1. What worked and is worth repeating?

2. What needs improvement?

While you may never again have to ask for a raise, you will, in the course of your lifetime, have many difficult conversations. By utilizing theatre strategies & soft skills (e.g. goal setting, preparation, and scriptwriting, public speaking, and stellar presentation) to prepare for the conversation — and framing the results with these two questions — you hone a *process*. This gives you the ability to move forward to the next difficult conversation. And the next, and the next, and so on.

In each chapter, we break down the subject skill. We'll discuss our definition of the skill, why it's vitally important to you, and how to build it or strengthen it.

At the end of each chapter, you'll find specific exercises or activities designed to grow your skills. You'll also find real life, honest-to-goodness examples of people successfully putting the particular (highlighted) skill(s) into practice. Seriously, the individuals in these scenarios are real, though we've changed the names to avoid having to pay them any money.

Now, if I know people (*and I know people*), that last bit about exercises and activities may have you grimacing and seriously re-thinking your life choices.

Good.

Change is hard. Personal growth and professional development require effort. If you want to make changes, *you actually have to make changes*. You can't keep doing the same things in the exact same way and expect different results.

Some might call that insanity.

One final thing to keep in mind before we crack this beast is that soft skills are human skills. They often blend together. So, while there is a chapter devoted to communication and conversation, there is a separate chapter on public speaking. These things are related and rely on one another, but we've broken them down to address very specific needs.

Okay, one *really* final thing...

Skills are built over time with small steps, small light-bulb moments, and tiny, conscious changes. Building skills is like building muscle — we have to create little micro tears in what exists so we can make it better, stronger and more useful. The world needs you not to be someone else, but to be the absolute freakin' best version of yourself that you can craft.

Now, on with the show.

Okay, I lied, here's the *really, really* final thing: Throughout the book you'll see little notes called "Cue Cards." I've set them apart because these are some of the biggest, most gorgeous, delicious nuggets you'll get from this book. So pay attention to them!

See, I saved you a highlighter.

Chapter 1:

What The Hell Are "Soft Skills" And Why The Heck Do I Need Them?

Excellent question.

We define soft skills as follows:

 The group of non-technical and/or interpersonal skills that act as the connective tissue between humans.

We like to call soft skills "the creamy center."

Actually, that's not true. Nobody says that.

9

Here's an example for clarification: Conversational competency — the ability to profitably hold and contribute to a conversation — is a soft skill because it requires two or more people speaking, listening and interacting with each other.

Calculus is not a soft skill, however, the ability to communicate mathematical findings or to work with others to solve mathematic problems, **IS** a soft skill.

Here's another example: Spelling the word "team" isn't something we would describe as a soft skill, however the ability to build a team of people who work well together, who can create together and who deal with conflict successfully, ranges the spectrum of soft skills.

It gets easier as we go along.

Although not exhaustive, here is a list of some of the most valuable soft skills that you can learn and develop:

Communication	Conflict mediation
Public speaking	Team building
Storytelling	Creative thinking
Active listening	Observation
Conversational competency	Etiquette (business and personal settings)
Negotiation	
Personal branding	Problem solving
Caretaking	Leadership skills
Goal setting	Sales
Emotional intelligence	Accountability & Self-awareness

And so on…

Soft skills make the world go 'round. Every great invention or step forward that ever was — or ever will be — happened because of the thinker's ability to communicate meaning to someone else. No person is an island, and innovation ultimately requires consensus.

That's why soft skills are the gold of the 21st century. Assuming we've not blown ourselves to bits and that we still have a habitable planet, jobs in 2030, 2040, and beyond will look wildly different than they do now. Consider that whole, large-scale industries have grown with the advent of "smart" technology. In the past 20 years, we've grown a vast array of new jobs to meet the technology revolution, while automating and "retiring" a plethora of others. Chances are, the jobs of the future might not even exist today, but people will.

The jobs of the future will require more communal problem solving, more critical and creative thinking and exceptional communication skills. That includes more of an ability to listen and empathize with the humans standing next to (and across) from you. We build technology for human use. Technology serves humans.

Well, until the machine uprising and then all bets are off, but that's a different movie.

At the intersection of humanity and technology are omni-skilled people. These are the people who have proficient "hard" or technical skills in their field, and they have the ability to speak about those skills. They can communicate in a variety of effective ways, ***and*** work with other humans using creative methods to collaborate and solve problems.

The trope of the brainy, yet stuttering nerd — who is too shy and awkward to speak — is now as outdated and outmoded as the charismatic jock airhead who can't tie their own shoe. These caricatures have no place in a 21st century workforce.

There's also the money component.

With data compiled from human resource studies, workforce and pipeline research, we know that people with greater soft skills make more money. We also know that companies are more profitable when they foster soft skills in their employees.

Let me say it again for the people in the back: <u>Soft skills have a direct monetary value.</u> We know this.

Think about what you want from your interactions with other people. You need your sales team to be observant, critical, and creative thinkers who can problem-solve on the fly. You want the customer service person on the other end of the phone to actually listen to and address your issue. We want our children to be able to interact well with others. We want to interview well to get our dream job, and to lead our teams with integrity and empathy to goal achievement.

This is the actual value of soft skills and why the hell you need them.

A key understanding before we move on: Soft skills are human/relationship skills.

Yes, you will make more money if you hone your skills because you have to work with other people. Consider also that you live with people, or maybe you want to live with people. You desire mutually satisfying relationships, even with your sister in Albuquerque, whom you can't stand.

You want to live an existence that is more than simply *surviving*. You want to *thrive*.

The more skills you have, and the better your skills are, the better you are at understanding yourself and the people around you. This is known as emotional intelligence (EQ). The better listener and communicator you become, the more observant and empathetic of human behavior you are. You'll also add more value to every single human interaction.

12

For example:

Scene #1: Laura, a fitness instructor and personal trainer, decided that she wanted to produce an event for women to create connection and community. The only problem was that she was terrified to speak in front of others. Her anxiety was paralyzing, and yet, she understood that the only way out, was through.

We explored what was driving her to put on the event, what her messaging would be, and what she wanted the audience to receive from her. Over a couple of months, she and I worked on her **public speaking** skills, her **word choices, branding and storytelling skills** and her ability to **fail forward**. The day of her event arrived, and while her anxiety was riding high, she was able to lean into the skills she had sharpened and put on a hell of an experience. Her event was so successful that she was asked to produce it again, and she plans to do more speaking events in the future.

Scene #2: Beth, an accountant at a medium-sized firm, had decided to run for public office in her town. Beth was not a person used to being in the spotlight, but was so gobsmacked by what she saw happening in her community that it compelled her to run. Not only did we work for long hours on her stump speeches, but we also had many conversations about **"value proposition"** — what she was uniquely qualified to bring to the table and how would she communicate those skills and ideas. We worked on **listening skills** and **general communication acuity**, how to breathe and take a **power pause** and a **power stance**, and how to offer thoughtful, off-the-cuff responses.

Unfortunately, Beth didn't win her race. She did, however, message me about two months later to let me know that she had been up for a review at her job. Because of our work together, she was able to speak confidently about her contributions to the firm (her value proposition), and ended up with a $15,000 raise. Hell yeah!

Scene #3: David was a support specialist at a software company. It was his job to talk to clients about how to use the software, functionality, and best practices. We worked together because he realized that his clients were not engaging with him in the way he wanted, and as a result, they weren't getting the best possible experience from the product. Together, we worked on his **storytelling skills**, and making him more relatable to his clients. David was able to develop better **listening and empathy skills**, which enhanced his **problem-solving abilities**. His manager took note of how David was improving himself, and promoted him to a more senior position. He now manages a **team** that reports directly to him.

Scene #4: In 2019, I delivered my first TEDx Talk. I spoke about the relationship between **confidence** and how we speak about ourselves **(personal branding)**. Essentially, by choosing to make better, more profitable word choices, we can reshape how we see ourselves and, in turn, how we interact with the world. Since that talk, I've received so many positive messages from people, both male and female, who are now more purposeful and powerful in their language. They've let me know how making those small changes has had a dramatic effect on their lives.

And that — plus a million other reasons — is why the hell you need better soft skills.

Chapter 2:

Everything Is Communication

Everything IS communication. No hyperbole. No hard sell here. Just naked, unadulterated facts.

When you learn to communicate well, the world changes. Vistas open, choirs sing and angels strum their tiny harps.

Okay, so maybe some hyperbole.

What we're mostly going to talk about in this chapter is personal, face-to-face, communication. Why we do it, what we get from it, and how to do it better and more profitably.

When we consider face-to-face communication, we're specifically talking about video conferencing, public speaking, networking, and general conversational situations. You know, your average life.

It's hard to know where to begin with *movie announcer voice* COM-MUNICATION, because it's such a broad topic. So let's start with a definition. The folks at **Merriam-Webster** have never let me down yet:

com·mu·ni·ca·tion | kə-ˌmyü-nə-ˈkā-shən

1. a process by which information is exchanged between individuals through a common system of symbols, signs, or behavior.

There are several things to unpack here.

First, communication is a process. It is not one single thing taken at one single time. It requires context. It is a compilation of the give and take of exchanges over a period of time, that may or may not lead to meaning.

Second, it's really important to understand that communication only happens when there is a commonly understood system. If you speak to me in Swahili, we're not communicating because we're not utilizing a system that is shared between us. George Bernard Shaw famously wrote, "The problem with communication is the illusion that it has taken place."

This second part is where the majority of miscommunication occurs. We think we're communicating in a common system, but even if you're speaking the same language, meaning may be hard to accurately define. Think about when you were confused by a word, a tone, or a facial expression someone used. Even a lack of response can be ambiguous. That's because...

Communication is imperfect and subjective to every single individual.

Doesn't that just make everything a hairy, ridiculous mess?!

Yes. Yes, it does.

On the bright side, it provides the expression of voice, color and uniqueness to each person. *Totally worth it.*

Understand this: Conversations about communication are imprecise. There is no dictionary of communication, and it's culturally specific — meaning that while we're going to discuss COMMUNICATION (again, with the movie announcer voice), the context is the United States in the 21st century.

Although, and as an interesting aside…

There is some evidence that the arms-above-the-head-I-win, gesture may be universal. Researchers have noted it in blind people, very small children and people living in geographically isolated areas. So go ahead and throw those hands up!

To consider great communication, we need to understand why we communicate.

 We communicate to SURVIVE, THRIVE & CREATE CHANGE.

We are social beasts. And, no, I'm not talking about how many "likes" or followers you might have on social media. We live in communal groups. Think of a bullseye, with yourself in the middle. The next ring is the people/family with whom you share a dwelling. That dwelling is probably in a city or town of some sort, which is the next ring. Your town is in a county, in a state, in the U.S. Our social and familial structures are much like these concentric circles.

Every reason you have to interact, engage, and communicate with any other person can be distilled down to the desire to survive, thrive or create change.

Humans evolved spoken language in order to convey data and meaning that, without which, we could not otherwise have prospered. Imagine our cave-dwelling fore-parents and their rudimentary language of clicks, grunts, gestures and postures. It was probably imperative for humans to develop language in order to perpetuate the species. Time, physical evolutionary changes and geography have all given rise to over 6,900 languages spoken around the world.

Okay, okay — we have a lot of languages! Most of them are spoken, (e.g. English, Swahili, and French), and some of them are not — (e.g. American Sign Language and Morse code). In communication with a spoken language, here's how humans do it:

Verbal - Spoken

Nonverbal - Physical/body language, proximity, appearance, eye contact, etc.

Paraverbal - The tone or energy with which words are spoken

The percentage of importance of each is still up for debate. We know that words, specifically, language, are a vehicle for data. We also know that humans begin assessing each other within seconds or milliseconds of becoming aware of each other — before any words are spoken. What is undeniable is that people will receive your message through their own filter. It's your job to be as clear, truthful, and authentic as you possibly can be.

Let's spend a moment and break these terms down. Walk with me...

Verbal

First, there's the spoken word. While words are the delivery system for facts and concepts, our word choices can tell people a lot about us.

Imagine if you will, a well. But instead of water, this well is filled with all the words you know and use. This well is built brick by brick from your upbringing, beliefs, education, cultural affinity, geography, experiences, and a thousand other stones that form your world view. The words in the well, made from all of these components, are a direct reflection of you as a person. There is importance and weight to those words, because words matter.

 The words you use, and how you use them, tell the world who you are.

I was having a conversation with Don, a guy in his early 50s. He's a handsome, personable, easy to get along with guy. During the course of this conversation, Don described to me a man he had met recently and he off-handedly described him as a "nerd." Suddenly, I had an insight into who Don was. I already knew that Don had been an athlete in high school. Not a great student, but popular and bright, and had a general good time of high school. When he used the word "nerd" to describe the acquaintance, I understood that Don still labeled people based on those high school categories — nerd, jock, freak, etc.

In telling me a story about someone else, Don revealed a bit about himself. This is the power of our word choices.

You get to choose the words you use.

You can be thoughtful and considerate to yourself and others with your words, or you can use them as bludgeons — designed to hurt and deconstruct. Words can build worlds, and they can destroy them.

Remember the old adage about sticks and stones breaking bones, "… but words will never hurt me?"

They lied, but you get to choose. Build or break — the choice is yours.

Nonverbal

I'm not going to lie — conversations about nonverbal communication are some of my favorites. They're so rife with "ah-ha" moments because most people don't realize the extent of what nonverbal communication entails. While social scientists continue to battle over what fraction of communication is delivered nonverbally, suffice it to say it's A LOT.

What do you think it is? Body language? Yep.

Eye contact? Sure is.

Facial expression? You betcha!

It's also clothing, proximity, touch, gestures, scent (yes, scent!), and so much more.

Consider your choice of clothing. You choose your clothes for a variety of reasons — comfort, design, occasion, etc. Clothing is an outward expression of ourselves. It basically tells the world who you are, or at least who you consider yourself to be. Clothing is a conversation.

Proximity is a conversation as well. Imagine riding an elevator with other people. We're all careful not to make too much eye contact, and certainly not to get too close to one another if it can be helped. We all have our "bubbles." If you've ever ridden a New York City subway at rush hour, you know what it is to be a sardine in a can — packed in tight with little or no personal bubble-space.

Imagine a virtually empty subway car. You just want to get home and finish watching the latest season of whatever you're binging on Netflix. You've got three stops to go before you're home. The train slides into the next station and a person gets on, and comes to stand right next to you. There is an entire, practically empty train car, and they're standing right next to you. It's weird. It's uncomfortable. They're in your bubble with no reason. It feels threatening because where we choose to place ourselves relative to other people is a nonverbal conversation.

Let's talk about scent for a moment.

Scent is an incredibly powerful nonverbal cue. Consider this…

Did you take a shower this morning with soap or body wash?

Cool, we're happy you did. Now, did you wash or condition your hair? Use a shave cream on your pits, legs or face?

Did you slick up with a face cream, body lotion or oil?

Did you put on deodorant? Again, thank you.

Did you splash or spritz on a bit of fragrance? Brilliant.

Now ask yourself if any of those things were "human scented?"

Probably not. Most likely, they were "gardenia island breeze" or "toasty coconut creme" or "fancy toilet water." The point is that we spend gazillions of dollars of our hard-earned money to not smell human.

Because scent is a nonverbal conversation. Scent is the sense most strongly tied to memory. Scent is primal. My unscientific guess is that every human on the planet is somehow triggered in our lizard brain by the scent of fire.

Scent stirs us, transports us, and can create actual changes in our brain chemistry.

Every Christmas Day, we would go to my grandmother's house in the morning. On the porch, we'd stamp the snow off our boots, and when we'd open the door, there was Grandma, wearing her Christmas apron, with smiles and hugs for everyone. Her little house smelled throughout of all kinds of muffins and breads she had been baking for days before. It remains one of my happiest memories, and to this day, whenever I bake blueberry muffins or banana bread, it makes me think of my Gram and Christmas morning.

Scent will get you every time.

There's the flip side as well. Again, imagine that same crowded subway ride. You squeeze in to find that the guy next to you, who insists on holding the pole above your head, hasn't used deodorant today.

Or maybe hasn't bathed at all.

In days.

Scent is a conversation.

Paraverbal

Paraverbals are a sort of sub-class of nonverbal communication. They aren't the words, but rather *the way we say words* — tone, cadence and pitch.

Paraverbals are an indicator of energy or emotion. When we're happy, excited, or playful, our voice may pitch higher. If we're tired, angry, or thoughtful, our voice may pitch lower.

Emphasis placed on certain words can entirely change the meaning of the conversation. Say these examples out loud, emphasizing the bolded words:

You're **NOT** going out dressed like that!

YOU'RE not going out dressed like that!

You're not going out dressed like **THAT**!

It's the same words, though the interpretation is vastly different. The conversation changes based on the inflection, and it's powerful stuff.

A final word on paraverbals. We humans make sounds that, linguistically, aren't actually words. Utterances like, "mmmm," or "humph," or a well placed grunt can provide real meaning to a conversation. These vocal interjections don't easily fall into a category of communication, so we're going to leave them right here under paraverbals.

As we said in the beginning, communication is everything. The totality of human skills rests on communication as a foundation. Not a small thing, and you'll notice that we'll circle back to this idea (and communication skills in general) throughout the rest of this book.

Get used to it. You're gonna have to learn to talk pretty.

Now that you understand the why and how of communication, let's get into communication strategies.

Let's Start With Communication Imperatives

First, and perhaps the most obvious imperative, is the necessity of the message. Don't talk just to hear yourself. Does anyone, anywhere ever want to sift through any form of communication to uncover the point of a message? Of course not! We humans are scrollers and swipers — we want to get to the point. Without a specific need, the entire conversation is a non-starter. We must make sure our message is succinct, distilled, and valuable.

The second and third imperatives relate to being the receiver of the message. The person to whom we're communicating must be willing and able to receive the information. Think of giving or receiving driving directions in a foreign language. There's a gap in ability for both the giver and receiver. It's an accident waiting to happen.

Here's another example: You ask someone to call you. You give them your phone number and yet, when they call, you don't answer your phone. You haven't put yourself in a position to receive the information you require.

Or, as we humans often do, we'll make a show of hearing the words someone is saying, but we're so busy planning what we're going to say next, we don't *listen* to the message. There is a huge difference between hearing and listening.

Hearing is passive. Listening is active and participatory. It means that you're taking in all of the communication cues the person is relaying.

Craft great communication by following the three imperatives:

- Create a message that is needed, valuable and concise.

- Position yourself to get the information you need.

- Actively and openly receive the information.

A Moment for Silence

Silence is a powerful communication tool, and we basically use it in one of two ways.

The first is a purposeful, powerful pause. Whether it be during a conversation or a keynote speech, we use silence strategically to create anticipation, to await a response, or to assert dominance. When we don't rush to fill the space with words, what we're left with is energy, and that energy is powerful.

The other side of silence is avoidance. We're silent because we're afraid, unsure or intimidated. So we avoid, withdraw, and don't respond.

Man, oh man, is it frustrating to be on the other side of that particular silence. It's a hard conversation.

Allow me a moment here...

We'll often beat our heads against someone's silence. We'll allow for broken phones, theoretical emergencies, too-busy schedules, lightning storms that took out the cell tower, and the zombie apocalypse.

What? It could happen.

It didn't though.

 People give their attention to what they want to acknowledge. The rest is noise.

NOT receiving a response IS a response, just not the one you wanted.

Moving on.

Knock, knock. Who's th... Interrupting elephant

We humans interrupt each other all of the time. We take it as a hall-mark of passionate conversation. The clean, clinical truth though is that when we interrupt someone, we *insert* and *assert* our point of view as more important than what the speaker is saying. We assume we already know what they were going to say, so we don't actually need to hear them say it. Then we interrupt with our nugget of golden truth.

It's the elephant in the room.

The assumption that we know *more* or better than the person we're speaking with.

Maybe you do. Maybe you have something brilliant to add to the conversation. Great! Here's what you do...

Stop talking.

I know, it's hard — what you've got to say is so good/right/zinger-y. Still, don't. It takes confidence to stop talking. It takes willpower and the possibility that what someone else is saying is as, or more important than, your need to interrupt in that moment.

When you interrupt or talk over someone, you've hijacked the conversation. You've taken control of a dialogue that perhaps wasn't yours to take. You've essentially told the person you're speaking with that what they have to say doesn't matter.

Imagine that someone else's point of view or experience is equally valid as yours, and just as important to them as yours is to you.

Listen to them. Listen not only to the words they're saying, but how they're saying them. What is their body language telling you? There are worlds to understand when you don't use the time that someone else is speaking to just formulate your next pithy bon mot and you actively listen.

 **For example:**

Scene #1: Several years ago, I had an eye opening experience with a family member. We had a disagreement based on something she had done, that had a direct negative effect on my life. I tried to talk to her, leaving several voice mails. No response. I texted her. No response. I direct messaged her on social media. She unfriended me.

I began to get the message.

While open dialogue and thoughtful communication are *very* important to me, they were less so to her, at least as it related to me, in this situation. Her silence was her response. The sound of crickets chirping was the conversation. It certainly wasn't the one I wanted, and it definitely wasn't the resolution I had hoped for, but there it was.

There was nothing left but to accept her response and move on.

Scene #2: I was at a lunchtime networking event, and it was the type of event where everyone has the opportunity to stand up and share their **Elevator Pitch**. It was my first time meeting this group of people, and they seemed receptive after I dazzled them with my theatre-strategies-based-communication-training-business pitch. Except for one guy.

He decided that there was nothing special about what I did — so much so that when he stood up to deliver his Elevator Pitch, he decided to sing a poem about frogs. As if his role as Sailor #2 in a high school production of *Anything Goes* 30 years ago provided him the skills that were necessary to do my job. You can't make this stuff up! I had no idea what his **imperative** was to sing/speak, or why he felt the need to disparage my work, but he did, and in doing so, he showed the group more about who he was than he could have ever told us directly.

Everything is communication.

 **Moving forward:**

To begin to understand the scope of what goes into exceptional communication skills, we're tasking you with an exercise that is <u>actively passive</u>.

Your job is to people watch, without judgement or expectation. Sit quietly in a park, a museum, a restaurant, or wherever you can observe people without being weird about it. Look at them interacting with each other. Notice how they lean into each other, touch each other, smile and speak to each other.

Listen not to the words, but to the pitch of their voices and how their emotions are telegraphed in the way they stand or move. Look at the way children move compared to adults.

Look, listen and observe. Do this for a half hour, with no distractions (silence your phone).

Then, write three observations about what you've seen, and what you imagined was happening in those moments with those people. The observations might look something like this:

1. Woman with a child attempting to walk quickly. Woman seemed frustrated and child didn't want to walk and was dragging his feet.

2. Young man and woman walking and eating ice cream. Lots of smiling and talking, but no touching. Friends? Maybe soon-to-be lovers?

3. Two women holding hands walking close together, in step. They seem comfortable.

The point is to be quiet and listen to the way people interact and with what energy, emotion and intention.

 The last, best communication advice you'll ever need: Speak less, mean more.

Chapter 3:

Hell Yes, the Words You Choose Matter!

Congratulations on making it to chapter three! You're clearly a brilliant thinker and an avid learner.

Enough with the schmooze, let's get going.

In this book, you've already read that words matter. You'll read it many more times before you turn the final page. That's because (and we can't emphasize this enough) *words do matter.*

The words you choose to use reflect and reveal you. They tell the world not just what you think, but how you feel about what you think.

 The words you use reflect your beliefs, your education and experiences, as well as your biases.

Words are not a small thing. It takes time and thoughtfulness to understand why we say the things we do, the way we do. Mostly, it takes a bit of self-awareness. Words are what show up on the surface, but they've bubbled up from very deep within us.

In this chapter I'm going to give you "word situations." These are instances where it's beneficial to have more word awareness. Instances where the words you use and/or how you use them can be improved. Not only for your benefit, but also for the benefit of everyone you ever speak with, speak to, or speak around; basically *ANNOUNCER VOICE* for the benefit of all human kind.

We're going to start easy and move into the more "rough" situations. Think constructive and destructive.

Verb'd Nouns

You read that right. It's now become acceptable in our world to add suffixes to the end of nouns in order to make it into an action word.

One of my personal favorites is "cocktailing" and not just because I love a good mojito, which I do.

Another one of my favorites is "ninjafy." I'd like to take credit for inventing this word, but apparently I did not, although my definition is absolutely better than the one listed in the Urban Dictionary[1]:

> *nin-juh-fahy* — the act of achieving goals in small, stealthy and unconventional ways, always moving toward a greater purpose.

---

1 6 Gig. "Definition of Ninjafy, #2." Urban Dictionary. February 17, 2003. https://www.urbandictionary.com/define.php?term=ninjafy

This is the kind of language that bonds us and reminds us that we belong to a certain social group. Remember, our definition of communication included using a common system of words. Our shared lexicon of verb'd words is reflective of our communication. So when you're asking me if I want to go cocktailing with you on Friday night, it's proof of our bonding. We're literally speaking the same language.

There's a great TED Talk by Dictionary Editor Erin McKean about verb-ing nouns, compounding and blending words. I highly recommend it and it's just plain fun.

Moving on.

Here's where we start to look at the dark side of our word choices.

Name-Calling

I'm just going to say it out loud: name-calling is one of the least profitable ways to use words. And it's just the worst.

Seriously, have you ever changed anyone's mind by name-calling?

"OMG Becky, you're absolutely right, I AM an asshole. Thank you for pointing that out to me. I'll get right to work on becoming less asshole-ish."

That never happens. Shocking, I know.

Name-calling is so much more about the speaker than the receiver. It's an expression of anger, frustration, and fear, particularly when we feel powerless. Think about when you're driving and another driver pulls a bone-headed move. Maybe you flip them the bird while shouting a hearty "asshole!" It's a reaction born of the fear of a crash. It accomplishes nothing. It doesn't even feel that good.

Name-calling is the power of the powerless. It achieves nothing.

Pause here for a moment...Consider how and when you've name-called, or been name-called. It hurts. It can create a long-term negative impact. And while I understand that there are many people on Twitter who make a living by throwing insults at people, I believe we can do better.

Name-calling does not solve a problem. Very often it makes everything worse.

Name-calling — even if it's not directly to a person, but about a person — is toxic, and falls into the category of "destructive" language. These are words, idioms, colloquialisms and situational sayings that are designed to hurt or *deconstruct* a person.

Yeah, here's where it really starts to get rough.

Destructive Language

If you think of excellent communication as building blocks, consider the things that erode those blocks. Name-calling is one.

Biased words are another. There are, inherent in our society, words that have evolved with connotations that are coded and/or biased. They exclude, demean, and mock people because of race, impairment, social standing, education and so on.

For example, the word "boy" in and of itself is unremarkable. However, if you're speaking to a Black man and you use the word "boy," the meaning is racially fraught and demeaning. In this situation, context is everything.

If you're speaking about your female supervisor and you choose to use the word "bossy" to describe her, we understand you're not offering up a compliment. In fact, you're attempting to tear her down.

These are words and uses of language that on the surface say one thing, but underneath are actually designed to undercut and/or to put the subject in their "place."

Here are a few examples of common uses of biased/coded language:

> Well, look at Carole, isn't she "feisty" (Meaning female, direct and/or assertive).

> Sheila, you're a good manager but a little too "bossy" (Meaning female, direct and/or assertive).

> I liked Donte for the position, but don't you think he's a little too "urban" (Meaning Black).

> The group of "thugs" ran down the street, into the crowd (Meaning Black people).

> The "middle class" in America is in decline (Meaning White people).

> Rush Limbaugh accused Michelle Obama of "uppity-ism" (Meaning Michelle didn't know her "place;" meaning Limbaugh was making a blatantly racist statement).

Are you beginning to get the picture?

If you're hiding behind certain words so that you can _mean_ something cruel or negative, while not actually saying something cruel or negative, you're still being destructive.

It costs you nothing to consider other people's point of view and to inject some awareness into your speech and writing.

How do we address these coded words? You give them back to the speaker.

Imagine the coded language as something physical you could hold in the palm of your hand. Imagine showing that language and pointing to the suspect word(s), and asking the speaker what they meant?

Yes, it's tough.

Yes, it's seriously uncomfortable.

And, yes, it has to be done in order to continuously move the conversation forward. Keep in mind, you cannot control what someone else says or does, but you can make them aware of the negative impact they're having.

And, if it's not inadvertent, if they know exactly what they're saying, you get the oblique pleasure of asking them to acknowledge the crappy thing they're saying.

Here's how to begin that conversation: "Well Bob, I am a good manager, and I'd like to understand what you mean by the word 'bossy'?"

Note that the conversation begins with an affirmative, then moves into the actual give-back using "and," never "but."

Chances are that the person will be rightly surprised at your question and will try to put it back on you — "What do you mean, 'What do I mean by "bossy?"'"

The conversation can go downhill quickly. It's up to you to keep calm and straightforward. "Well Bob, 'bossy' has a negative connotation. I'd like to understand what specifically you mean by that word?"

Does this conversation sound implausible or impossible? It's not. I've taught hundreds of people to use a variation of this dialogue.

Don't enter the conversation with a "gotcha" attitude. Look for understanding, whether it's yours or theirs.

Name calling and coded and/or biased words are both examples of destructive or deconstructive language.

For a long time, I let the destructive words of my upbringing shape me, literally and figuratively. Walking to the lakeside beach on a sunny, summer day and having my dad shout out to me, "Hey Crisco…! Yeah, I'm gonna call you Crisco, 'cause you're fat in the can…" was mortifying and hurtful. He thought it was funny. He thought he had made a great joke.

My fragile 13-year-old self did not find it funny.

Years later, my dad apologized for this and other comments, but only after I made it clear that what he brushed off as "jokes" weren't, and that he had caused real pain.

Words matter.

Limiting, Qualifying or Justifying Language

This language is self-destructive. These are words and phrases we use when writing or speaking that take away from us, that excuse the space we take in the world, and that, ultimately, make us small.

They deliberately and insidiously subtract from our skills, abilities and our singular awesomeness.

It must stop RIGHT NOW.

Here are some examples of limiting language:

"I'm no expert, but could we maybe do it like this?"

"Maybe I'm wrong but how about XYZ thing?"

"I'm sorry but I don't understand what you're talking about."

 Think simple, declarative statements and questions.

"Can we do it like this?"

"How about XYZ thing?"

"I don't understand what you're talking about."

There is absolutely no need to frame yourself as *less than*. It serves no one and it undermines your language, your position and your perceived value to the situation.

Have you ever used "just" in the opening of a conversation or an email?

"Hi Bob, I'm just calling to see if you received my proposal?" As if you literally have to justify why you're taking up space/time/air.

You don't. *Tell them* why you're calling or emailing, *don't justify why.*

"Hi Bob, I'm calling to see if you received my proposal." It's a question and a statement. We could take that further and simply say, "Hi Bob, did you receive my proposal?" I personally like the social lubrication of saying the words "I'm calling" rather than launching right into "Did you receive my proposal?"

But you do you.

Either way, there's a big difference in position by omitting a small, unnecessary word.

Are you overwhelmed by all the word choices? That's okay.

Put this book down. Get a snack. Watch a video. Walk your dog. Come back later, Sparkles, I'll still be here for you.

Constructive Language

Words are not apathetic. Every word you speak, you've chosen to speak; whether they tumble out of your mouth in a mudslide, or you've deliberated as if your very life depends on what you say next.

Given that choice, why not choose to consciously be more constructive with your words? Following are four ways you can begin to rewrite your word choice scripts:

1. **Think "could" instead of "should."** The word should is exhausting. It's jam-packed with guilt and judgement. It's the verbal equivalent of a dirty, weighted blanket. BUT, if you begin to consider what you "could" do (see what I did there?!), you'll see that it opens vistas of possibilities.

Positive, constructive possibilities.

2. **Become an improv artist and use "Yes, and..."** The first and most fundamental tenet of improvisation is you can never say "no." Regardless of what ridiculous, impossible and outlandish thing your scene partner comes up with, your response is always to accept it and build on it with "Yes, and..." It would be impossible for me to overstate the benefit of utilizing "Yes, and..." in conversations, particularly difficult ones.

Here's the kicker — It doesn't have to mean agreement. It's an excellent way to let the other person know that you've listened and heard what they said. You're willing to be open to an idea, even if it's a starting point.

That makes you a hero.

For example:

Bob: "...and that's my idea on how we use mayonnaise to stop global warming!"

Bob's manager: *Pause* "Yes, and I really appreciate that you're thinking outside the box. Kudos to you, Bob. Does anyone else have any outside the box ideas?"

3. **Stop using words like "always" and "never."** Speaking in absolutes diminishes your argument and they're rarely, if ever, true. Like, ever...

4. **Consider your "but"(s).** Not to be confused with "butts."

In this situation, we're talking about a "but" in the middle of the sentence, which completely derails what your audience hears. For example, "this is a perfect proposal, *but* could you change this one little thing?" Soooo, it's not perfect and all we hear is you want changes. Using "but" suggests that only one thing is true, while "and" allows for multiple options.

Or, "I love you, but I'm leaving." Ouch!

 Everything before a "but" goes away after the "but."

"I AM" Statements

Can we talk about how much I freakin' love "I AM" statements, because they are positive and affirmative and joyful?!

Outside of drafting your resume, how often do you consider what you're good at — where your skills and abilities lie? How often do you think, "I am really good at this particular thing?"

How often do you actually say what you're good at, to yourself? Or, to other people, out loud?

Infrequently?

Seldom?

Never?

Well, the time is now. What are you good at? Where/what is your talent, regardless of how small or weird you may think it is?

You make gorgeous custom tailored felt jackets for your cat, Winky? Brilliant!

You can rewrite any software program so that a specific order of keystrokes invokes a Chupacabra? Fantastic!

You can meditate for 10 minutes and change your mood? Spectacular!

You sing to your vegetables and they grow more, bigger? Stunning!

Do you even know how ridiculously, incredibly wonderfully awesome you are?

You don't need anyone's permission to be your fully incredible self. You absolutely don't have to worry about being "arrogant" or "full of yourself" if *what you're saying is true and accurate.*

I am an excellent writer. It's not arrogant, it's a fact.

I am an inspiring keynote speaker. Again, true.

I am a spectacular dancer. Questionable, but in the range of acceptably true.

 Your interior dialogues shape your exterior conversations.

The words we say to ourselves shape what we tell the world, and how the world will see us. Give us your best by giving yourself your best.

Speak well to yourself by knowing what skills, abilities, talents, leanings, and aptitudes you posses. Then, speak them to yourself.

Write them down. Make a lifelong list of all the cool things you can do and are good at. This is a gift for yourself, and you deserve it.

Then, begin speaking them out loud.

I have an email framed on my office wall from a client, Emma, who wrote to tell me that when she was in middle school, another girl accused her of thinking she was "all that." Emma said that she rushed to tell the girl that she did not think she was all that.

Imagine believing that you have to defend the idea that you're value-less.

And yet, how many of us do that in some form every day?

That's why "I AM" statements are so important. For many people, women in particular, thinking and believing a strong, positive "I AM" statement is an act of creation. It's epic. It's God-like.

Saying it out loud is an act of rebellion.

More on that later.

Always, always consider the words you use and why you use those particular words. The world will thank you.

 **For example:**

My friend Bob was recounting a story to me of a conversation he was having with another male friend of his. The conversation centered on something that Bob was willing to do, but his friend was not. During the exchange, Bob told me that he was "busting" on his friend, and teasing him that he was afraid to do the thing. Bob told his friend he was a "pansy" and they both laughed and carried on with the conversation.

After Bob recounted the story to me, I asked him if he thought there was anything wrong with using the word "pansy." He said no, and that he was just joking around. Bob also stated that he "...didn't mean anything by it..." But he did.

Pejoratives — like "pansy" or "pussy" — or any of a hundred others, are words rooted in homophobia, misogyny, and racism. These words also lean into the role of the superior "macho" man, and are destructive and hurtful. Don't let them in to your head or your space.

 **Moving forward:**

This is a big chapter with a lot of heavy stuff, so here's how you begin implementing these word rebellions:

Digest and then re-read this chapter. Then...

1. Begin becoming aware of what you say and how you say it. Start by listening to yourself and paying attention to others with a discerning ear — are you/they speaking in a constructive or destructive way? Write down examples of constructive and destructive language you use and that others around you use.

2. How do you/they speak about themselves? About others? Engage in conversations with others about the words they're using and how they make you feel (or how your words make them feel). Use the examples from #1 to jump-start those conversations.

Remember, tough conversations are the most profitable, and communication is subjective. What might not seem destructive to you may seem so to others.

Thoughtfully implement your improved word/language choices and observe how those changes create change in you and the world around you.

3. Finally, write down your skills. Write your abilities. Write out what makes you excellent. Then, ask your friends what they're good at — give them the ability to say it out loud. Initiate those conversations. Make space for you and them by actually *creating* the space.

What you'll gain by doing these exercises is a real world awarenesses of the power of your words, and the power of the words used in your universe.

Carry on word warrior.

Chapter 4:

If Nothing Else, Read This Chapter on Public Speaking

Public speaking is one of the most profitable job skills to put on your resume.

I know, I know. We all have a lot of feelings when it comes to public speaking. Usually those *feelings* are some mixture of dread, nausea, anxiety and a desperate need to locate the nearest exit.

What if — and stay with me here a moment — what if I told you that you've probably been "public speaking" your whole life, and just never realized it?

What if I also told you that by ramping up the public speaking skills you already have, you can make more money, grow in your position and more capably craft the life you want?

It's all true.

First, let me tell you how I define public speaking, because you might be surprised...

 Speaking to two or more people at a time is public speaking.

Yep, that's it.

Ever raised your hand in class, or worse, got called on and had to answer a question? Yes, that's public speaking. Have you attended an event where you gave an elevator pitch? That, too, is public speaking.

Have you ever offered an idea or feedback in a meeting? Bingo!

Have you ever had a conversation with two other people? You got it — public speaking. And again, you've been doing it your whole life and have a skill set you didn't realize you had. Granted, these are small instances but you're still speaking in front of others.

The technical term for the terror you might feel while speaking in public is called **evaluation apprehension**. In a nutshell, the more eyes that are on us, the greater the anxiety we might feel. The larger the group, the more pressure to perform.

So, how can we ratchet up our public speaking skills?

The short answer is conversation and confidence. There is a long answer, but for the moment, let's break down the conversation part.

Great communicators and public speakers understand that everything is a dialogue. <u>Even when one party isn't actually speaking, there is still</u>

a conversation happening. Refer back to **Chapter 2: Everything Is Communication**. When you're speaking, and your message is being heard, your audience is nodding, smiling, agreeing and providing other non-verbal cues of connectedness.

To be clear, lecturing is not public speaking. Lecturing (that is, reciting data without regard to the audience) is a monologue, and can be exactly the same whether anyone is in the room or not. Conversation begins by understanding to whom you're speaking. What is it you wish to communicate to this particular group of people and why?

This is where public speaking begins — the conversation.

The confidence part is much, *much* trickier.

It's hard to stand up in front of people. It's hard to put yourself out there. It's scary and naked-feeling.

You have to do it anyway and keep doing it. We'll build much more on this confidence component a bit later in the chapter.

Now, here's how we're going to break down the public speaking monster that lives under your bed and in your nightmares:

1. Audience

2. Mechanics - preparation, movement, engagement, breathing and anxiety

3. Environment

4. Something will go wrong

5. Confidence/bravery/authenticity

6. Speaking on/moderating a panel

1. Audience

Who is the audience, otherwise known as the people awaiting the next pearl of wisdom to drop from your lips? Who are they? Do you know to whom you are speaking?

If you're hanging with your friends, hopefully you have an excellent idea of who they are, (third-grade art paste eaters), what is important to them (e.g. work, a good handbag and their life partner — not necessarily in that order), and what topics are off limits (e.g. you are not allowed to discuss politics or the Willy Wonka remakes).

But what about the other audiences that you may not be so comfortable speaking with/in front of? Who are they, and how do you effectively speak to them?

It begins with your impetus to speak. Understanding what is driving you to speak to *this particular group* of people, will help to clear the road for real engagement, connectedness and communication. I once had an acting teacher who taught me that every movement, every moment on the stage must be life or death, *or don't do it.* His point, to put a fine tip on it, is this — if your reason for speaking/moving/being is not strong and clear, then what the hell are you even doing there? You're wasting my time. His words, not mine.

Harsh? Yes. 100% correct? Yes.

Know who you're talking to. What do they want from you? What did you promise you'd give them?

 Why MUST you speak? Why MUST you speak TO THESE PEOPLE?

Whether you're speaking to a stadium of 10,000 people or a boardroom of 12, understand that you're not speaking because you like to hear yourself, but because the audience absolutely must have the information you're giving them. This is the imperative. Call it whatever you like — drive, passion, or impetus. Serve the audience in the way that only you can.

Another key thing to understand about audiences is that your message can be inherently the same across a very wide audience scope.

For example, let's say you're giving a talk regarding the collateral benefits of kindness. If you're talking to workplace groups, you might offer statistics and facts about the chemical effects in the brain when we do something nice for someone else. You might talk about how kindness is a skill to be cultivated in leaders. You might open a philosophical dialogue with the audience about the nature of altruism.

Now imagine talking about kindness with an auditorium full of elementary school children. Your core message on the benefits of being kind to others remains the same, but your audience has changed dramatically. In order to engage this particular audience, you have to provide immediately relatable material. Maybe you talk about Santa Claus's kindness. Statistics won't necessarily work with this crowd, but you can ask them questions and expect to get a LOT of responses. When you share with them stories about who was kind to you and how, they will rush to tell you who was kind to them. And who wasn't.

Same topic, same overall message provided in two completely different ways.

Knowing exactly to whom you're speaking is one of the hallmarks of a great public speaker. When you know your audience, you are relatable and you create a rapport. You're speaking the same language and you are memorable in the best possible way.

Remember, we don't speak to be forgotten.

A last bit about audiences: What you give them and what they receive are entirely different things.

People are universes unto themselves, full of experiences, filters and points of view that we (individually) cannot begin to recreate. So why would we think that everyone would see, taste, feel, hear and ingest exactly as we do? It's not possible and yet, understanding that chasm of subjectiveness opens up other worlds of empathy and comprehension.

In working with clients preparing to produce their first big event or keynote, this give/receive paradigm is always an evolving conversation. Understand that *what we want them to have* is undeniably different from *what they will actually take away*. Of course, a handout is a handout and if you've offered them a white paper on "Six Ways to Build a Bigger Purple Widget," then that's exactly what they'll get.

We're not talking about the tangible hard goods. What we're talking about is more ephemeral and is the meat and potatoes of great public speaking. It's the information *and* ideas delivered with energy/zeal/confidence that become your message. It's also your particular you-ness.

Wrapped up in all of this is our own very particular brand of fear, insecurity and anxiety. When it comes to public speaking, we sometimes let those fears stand in the way of being the best possible speaker we can be.

One client, a real estate professional, was loath to speak about her achievements for fear of seeming "arrogant." She was about to speak in front of her peers from across the country, and it was appropriate and necessary to provide context for her bona fides. She needed to set the table for them so they could choose what they needed from her in order to buy in to her. We worked hard at making her comfortable and confident speaking about her accolades in a way that still felt authentic.

Another client, a fitness trainer, producing her first event for women in her community, wanted to "prove to women…" and show them what they "should be doing…" We honed her script so it was less about lecturing than offering an alternative choice. Once we found the right words, the entire presentation started to fall in line because she was able to step back from what she wanted her audience to walk out the door with, and relax into what she was providing to the audience.

The importance of word choices cannot be overstated.

Ultimately, people will receive what they're open to receiving. Sometimes you get very lucky and your audience will walk out your door having received something you couldn't have fathomed giving them. Enjoy that glorious moment! Your presentation shouldn't be a static thing. Learn from every opportunity for feedback and constantly evolve.

It's your job to prepare and to hone your presentation. To fill it with as much tactical information as well as personality, inspiration, aspiration, and energy that the time and space will contain. Then, let it go because the second after you speak, your presentation no longer belongs to you — it belongs to the audience.

2. Mechanics - preparation, movement, engagement, breathing and anxiety

The "mechanics" of public speaking are the things personal to us that we can control. Your mastery of each of these facets will do more to determine your effectiveness as a public speaker than any of the other topics combined. No pressure…

    a. Of course we'll talk about **preparation** first, because it is first, last and everything in between.

PREPARATION will determine if you succeed or fail as a speaker. Period.

I know there are speakers who "wing it."

Cool, cool. Don't be that guy.

You be you, and your best speaker-self begins with preparation. Understand who is in the audience, and what you need to say to them, in what format, in what time frame. These are all things that will shape your speech.

Write it out. Edit it. Edit it again. And again.

Read it. Again. Out loud. With an accent. Read it upside down and with green eggs and ham. Read it to your family and friends. The point is to hone your message, so that nothing is lost and there is nothing extraneous. Distill and distill until you get to the gorgeous lotus hiding within the muck.

A note on memorization: Many speakers memorize their talks or speeches. The problem with that is if you get thrown ('cause that never happens…) or you forget a line, you may end up crashing the entire gig. It doesn't have to be that way.

Here's what's better than memorization: Making your talk *organic*. This is a theatre concept. It means that you've rehearsed and practiced and sang and danced your words so many times; that you know in your bones, on which word you're going to breathe and move and pause, that it all becomes part of your DNA.

Here's the real beauty of making your speech organic — it allows for the inevitable "*something*." The "something" is the thing we can't control. Maybe your technology fails ('cause that never happens...), or you stumble on the stage, or someone snaps a flash photo of you during your talk and you forget your own name. Anything can happen to trip you up, literally or figuratively.

By making your talk organic, you can recover, adjust, adapt and keep moving forward — giving your audience the thing that they absolutely, positively can't live without — you!

One final word about being organic: If you've ever seen the same live show twice, whether a play, poetry reading, or musical event, you know you haven't actually seen the exact same show twice. While the words, lyrics or movements may have been the same, the energy was different. The mood or the tone are all different. Someone may have goofed or been especially in the zone. Moments are ephemeral. That's why preparation is paramount and live theatre blazes with energy.

b. Within preparation, comes **movement.**

I am frequently asked about gestures and movement, as in, "when should I move, or should I copy this other speaker's gesture?" Here's the thing, folks. Movement is part of your preparation and should become organic.

Remember we talked a while ago about your impetus to speak? Okay, it was like two pages ago, anyway, it's like that.

 MOVEMENT should always be purposeful.

When you're rehearsing, practicing and distilling, you should be doing it all on your feet. We do this to get a feel for the rhythm of the language we're using, to find the pauses, and the opportunities to engage with our audience.

For example, if you're on a large stage, you may want to find moments in your talk that drive you to move and engage with one side of the audience and then the other. This works particularly well if you're enumerating a list of items, or offering differing points of view.

By using the language and the movement to drive each other, rather than thinking, "well, this is a good time to shuffle over here..." you create energy, interest and engagement with your entire audience.

If you're presenting to a small room with only a few people, you can still accomplish this by turning your body slightly to make sure that you're front-facing all sides of the room.

Nobody, ever, at all, wants to watch someone stand in the middle of a space and recite something from memory, looking like it hurts them to be there. The exception is your baby cousin's 2nd grade history pageant.

Also, for the love of all that is good in the world, keep in mind that nobody *ever* wants you to read your slideshow presentation. It's lazy and it's death to the audience.

Find gestures and movement in your text that add to and underscore the drama of your narrative. Remember, public speaking is always a conversation. Movement is another way to engage with your audience.

We want (particularly if we've paid money) someone who is excited to give us the knowledge and stories we've come to see — in a professional and skillful way. No flailing of limbs. No "step, step, step, turn and repeat" across the stage. And absolutely no hands in the pockets. And absolutely, positively, no shuffle from leg to leg, regardless of when your last bathroom break might have been.

Again, take your hands out of your damn pockets. Here's some public speaking gospel for you: The only reason we put our hands in our pockets during a speech or talk is because we're uncomfortable, and putting our hands close to our genitals is a way of self-soothing.

It's 100% true.

And now you'll never look at anyone with their hands in their pockets the same way again, will you?

   c. There are hundreds of ways for you to create **engagement** with your audience.

You're not lecturing without regard to the audience. You're having a conversation in which one side is the primary speaker. Engagement is baked right into that cookie.

When you're practicing, think about where you can pause to check that the audience is with you. Ask yourself if you're making eye contact with audience members. What does their body language look like? Are they leaning in and nodding or, *gulp* are they checking their phones, while doodling and inching toward the door?

 It's up to you, the speaker, to create engagement opportunities.

A *good* public speaker tells an interesting story that holds the audience's attention. A *great* speaker brings the audience with them on the journey.

It's important to know this idea pertains to every subject anyone can speak about. You —the speaker — give the topic weight, humor, drama, whimsy, etc. It's you. It's all you and how you tell the story. This is true for a stadium-sized presentation as well as a small team meeting. It's true whether you're in the same room with your audience or everyone is on a video chat.

However you can connect with your audience in a positive way, do that!

I'm a giant fan of humor. I couldn't teach without it. In my workshops, it opens the door for participants to loosen up, to breathe and to laugh at me, themselves and each other in a supportive way.

Every single talk I've ever given, regardless of how large or small, has utilized humor. Whether it's an actual bad joke, a ridiculous fact or some over-the-top observation. I lay the groundwork from the first moment that we're here to play and build, and fail and rebuild.

Getting your audience's buy-in can include you asking them a question and waiting for a response. It can mean you respond to their response. It's electric and immediate.

I discovered a few years ago (completely by chance) how much humans love rewards, no matter what the reward. As it happens, I was shopping for supplies for an upcoming event, and found some glittery, puffy heart and star stickers. I'm not sure what made me buy them except that THEY WERE GLITTERY, PUFFY HEARTS AND STARS!

Anyway, during the event and on a lark, when a participant answered one of my questions correctly, I offered him a glittery, puffy star. He immediately put it on his event badge, as proud as if he had just won the 7th grade spelling bee. From that moment on, everyone competed for hearts and stars. They all leaned in a bit more, participated, and focused a bit more. We all laughed as we understood that the reward was just a sticker, but it didn't make getting it any less important.

It was exciting and very fun for everyone in the room. And, it created a spectacular avenue of engagement.

Ask your audience questions. Check in with them periodically, asking them if they agree or disagree with your point. Ask them to ask you questions. Tell a joke. Create interactiveness in some form.

By purposefully finding moments to interact and engage with your audience, they'll get more from you and you'll have a better time delivering. AND you'll become a better speaker.

    d. **Breathing and anxiety** are seemingly the most uncontrollable of controllable mechanics.

They're not.

Not when we learn to identify and reframe the things that are causing us stress and anxiety. When we can do that, we can utilize specific techniques to examine and become aware of the fears and limiting beliefs capturing us.

We all have limiting beliefs. They're those nasty little scripts we run in our heads that point to our myriad of faults, our shortcomings, and our past mistakes. This is where so much stress and anxiety comes from. Pointing at things that we think we'll mess up or fail at doing, as if the future was already written.

First, we have to recognize that we're running one of those negative scripts. Our self-trash-talk usually begins with, "I can't…" or "I'm not…" Recognize it, and ask yourself "why?"

"Why do I think this way?"

 Often, anxiety is rooted in the past.

This anxiety forms when we project what has happened in the past onto the future. And, as of this writing, we can't yet time travel and change the past, so we have to accept whatever *was*. AND we get to decide what will be.

This is where we begin to reshape and rewrite those scripts. This is where you grow your confidence. Looking forward — not backward — is the key.

Yes, it's nerve-racking and your heart is going to pound with each step closer to the scary thing. What if you fall/fail/screw-up? Again?

What if, indeed?

I'll let you in on a secret…we're all failures.

Every single person alive is a failure. We've all risked and failed, multiple times. Thousands of times. The story of your life is a story of failures. Mine too! There is no success, no reward, no life, without failure. We are all once and future failures. And that is a good thing.

You probably can't remember learning to feed yourself, but you can bet it was a hot mess. Poking yourself in the eye with a spoon, strained carrots in the hair, spaghetti everywhere and more food in your space than in your mouth. You failed until you didn't.

So you have options.

You can live with the anxiety and fear, and negative self-talk because it's comfortable. Because you've lived with it for a long time. You can count on it. It's part of you. And you can be stuck in the concrete of your limiting beliefs, OR…

You can be scared and step forward. You can examine the whys of your fear and choose to do something different. You can step up and step out of the concrete on to a new path.

Growing confidence requires action. Confidence-building is not a passive thing that "happens" because you want it to be so. Confidence is rooted in the falling down and getting up. It is acknowledging the process of "becoming." Bravery and letting go of past failures are the food of future confidence. As always, growing confidence requires consistently asking ourselves the same two questions: What worked and is worth repeating, and what needs improvement?

One of the tools I use on/for myself and with every single client is the actor's "what if?" I know, you're thinking that you "what if…?" yourself into terrible thoughts all the time, so how can that be helpful?

What if you put aside preconceived notions, hmmm?

The key is not to stop at the terrible thought where you fall off the stage, or fumble the winning touchdown or accidentally burn off someone's hair with a curling iron. The key and the benefit is to consider exactly what happens in the next moment, and next and next and next. We'll dig into this idea later in this chapter when we discuss bravery.

I'm interrupting this bit on anxiety to breathe.

Seriously, take a long, deep breath in. Now let it out.

There are a couple of breathing techniques I use and teach in many of my workshops. Both of these give you the ability to center yourself, slow the building anxiety, and help you feel more present and confident in the moment.

1. **Empty breath:** Breathe in as you would normally and then slowly exhale. Try to push as much air out of your lungs as possible. Hold for two seconds and then breathe as you normally would.

2. **Square breathing:** Visualize a square and begin at the top left point. At each of the following instructions, imagine you're moving along a side of the square until you return to start. Inhale for four seconds, then hold for four seconds, exhale for four seconds and hold for four seconds, returning to start.

Another way to combat anxiety and stress is to figuratively be your own superhero.

Whether you're Captain Clean or The Word Warrior, or even The Great Banana Avenger, adopting the posture of a superhero can have a profound effect on your brain chemistry.

Behold the "Wonder Woman" stance. Stand with your feet shoulder-width apart, hands on your hips, and take a few centering breaths. This posture has been scientifically proven to increase your serotonin levels and make you actually feel more calm and confident. In some of my workshops we call this "chin up and tits out." We like to laugh.

Go ahead, try it. Stand up. Assume the position. Breathe. Stay here for a moment reveling in your confident awesomeness.

That's right, you rock.

When we're stressed, we tend to contract our body, making it constrict and tighten inward. We begin to breathe quicker and with more shallow breaths. This chain reaction means that you're allowing less oxygen to process through your system, forcing you to breathe faster and making you feel more stressed and out of control, and certainly less confident.

Remember in the first chapter how we talked about making small changes based on becoming aware of behaviors? Adopting this posture is a small way to grow your awareness of your inner life and boost your confidence.

You can halt your stress cycle by stopping, standing and superhero-ing.

To be clear, I don't recommend doing this while speaking. It's weird. However, you can take a conscious pause with a deep breath, lifting your chin, and affirm a connection with your audience. That's a thing of beauty.

3. Environment

There are two components to the environment — controllable and uncontrollable.

a. Controllable

This is the obvious stuff. As part of your preparation (again, rehearse and prepare!), the onus is on you to investigate the space in which you're speaking. You need to know things like:

- how many people will be attending?

- how will the amplification system be set up (mics)?

- where is the stage/dressing room/restroom?

- where will you be before and after speaking?

- what time will you be speaking?

- will there be a rehearsal or can you set up prior to the event?

- how will the technology work, etc.?

It's your job, regardless of the gig, the event, the production, no matter how large or how small, to find out as many of these structured environmental items as you can. Obtaining this knowledge is part of your professionalism and allows you to deal with the uncontrollable and unknown.

If it's your event, you get to decide on the set up, the temperature, the lighting, the food, etc. Again, all of this is part of your preparation.

As we all know, regardless of how well you prepare, how many precautionary measures of forethought you've taken, there is an "X factor."

b. **Uncontrollable**

Technology will fail. The mic that worked perfectly at the sound check 20 minutes ago will break. People will be rude and talk on their phones while you're speaking. Waitstaff will drop a giant tray of dishes.

Shit happens.

I was running a public speaking class in a swanky hotel conference room. The room was set up exactly as I wanted. The lights, technology, and air conditioning were all working to perfection. I was just about to introduce my next module, when out of nowhere, the groundskeepers began mowing the grass right outside the room we were in. There was nothing to do but wait it out. So, while I smiled and waived at the nice man doing the mowing, I encouraged my participants to enjoy some refreshments and stretch their legs.

Again, shit will always happen. You have to control whatever is in your power to control, and roll with the rest.

SIDE NOTE: It's far easier to roll with the uncontrollable when you have a handle on the things that are within your power. Rehearse and prepare, people!

4. Something will go wrong

Recovering from a goof, no matter whose it is, is a skill. Trust me on this one!

During 7th grade chorus practice, I volunteered to give our instructor the "thank you" flowers after our concert that year. The evening of the concert arrived, and as we filed on stage to our pre-assigned riser, I carefully stashed the bouquet behind the tallest row of students and headed to the front where the latitudinally challenged singers were placed.

It was a terrific night and I sang my heart out. I was ready with my little gratitude speech, and after the last song, I stepped forward to deliver the goods… except, I froze. Literally… could not move, speak or think. The audience went from smiling and clapping to uncomfortable whispers. It wasn't until someone behind me, pushed me forward that I was able to unstick my feet, run around the risers, grab the flowers, throw them at the teacher and run off stage to cry and vomit on my new shoes.

It's a true story.

I'd like to tell you that ever since that fateful night, I've never made a mistake like that again.

I'd like to, but I can't.

Public speaking, in all of its forms, is live theatre, and in live theatre, something will always go wrong. Sometimes it's not even a question of "go wrong" so much as "be different than you planned."

Every client I've ever had asks basically the same question, "what if I forget what I'm supposed to say?" Well, my friends, here's the thing: It's not an IF, it's a WHEN.

IT WILL HAPPEN. The key — and what makes a great public speaker — is recovery. It's not the moment you lose it that matters, but what you do in the moment *after* that is the mark of excellence.

As an actor, I have absolutely blanked on my next line... during a show... in front of a packed house. It's terrifying, horrifying and holy-shit-able, and I survived. Every actor who has ever done any live theatre can attest, you will "go up." You will forget. It will happen. You will survive.

How will you handle it?

If your mic cuts out, you had better figure out how to continue while the AV people scramble to fix the issue.

If your projector overheats and turns off, do you know your material well enough to continue without those prompts?

Here's some advice on how to hone your goof recovery skills:

a. **Rehearse**

Don't allow technology to be your crutch. You're the draw. You're the one we want to hear. Slides and pictures are the gravy to your pork chop. Be the pork chop we need.

b. **Breathe**

Seriously, breathe. Remember how good breathing is for you and your brain.

I've seen speakers freeze and hold their breath. Or they are so anxious they start to hyperventilate. No good comes from that. One fellow I saw actually passed out. Allow yourself the space and the time to breathe. The audience may see it as a dramatic pause, and you can use it to run down mentally where you are in the scheme of things.

c. Use movement

This is an actor's tool. If you're not standing behind a podium with your notes at hand, take a breath, take a beat and move across the space. Often, the act of moving and gesturing will remind you of where you were and what's next. And once again, the audience may see it as a dramatic moment.

d. Use humor

If you're seriously lost and can't remember what comes next, bring the audience in on the joke. Admit you've lost your place while you check your notes. Be calm and the audience will relate and hopefully laugh with you. Humor is the best way to recover, from ANY goof, hands down. It creates rapport and gives a shared, relatable moment between you and your audience.

 Humor is the greatest goof recovery skill.

Arm yourself with the understanding that no event ever goes exactly as planned. You can capitalize on the goofs and gaffs and make the event, regardless of how small or large, more memorable than it would have if it had gone perfectly. This is the hallmark of an excellent speaker.

5. Confidence/bravery/authenticity

Hopefully, if you've made it this far in the chapter, you understand that confidence is a recipe made of many ingredients.

You have to rehearse, you have to breathe, you have to move, and you have to laugh. You must learn to control everything you can and make mental space for the thing(s) that will go wrong.

You have to sit with yourself, perhaps through a dark night of the soul, and rewrite the negative scripts that are stopping you from moving forward.

You need to have a reason to speak. What is your impetus? Why can you not speak?

Mostly, you have to do the thing. You have to speak. In order to get good at public speaking, you have to speak publicly. And, IT'S SO SCARY!

Remember earlier when we touched on the actor's "what if?" Here's how you use it for good instead of terror. Here's where a little actor's improvisational tool could change your life.

This is an excerpt from an actual conversation with a client about her upcoming public speaking event:

Client: I'm worried that I'll forget everything I want to say.

Me: Okay, what if that happens? When you are introduced, you stand up to speak, and nothing comes out?

Client: I stand there and people look at me...

Me: Yep, they're going to stare. And it'll be terrible. What if they stare? What if they throw fruit?

Client: They won't throw fruit.

Me: Of course they won't, so what will when do when they are staring and expecting you to speak?

Me: Will you run away?

Client: No.

Me: Will they boo you off the stage and immediately demand their money back?

Client: I don't think so.

Me: So *then* what will you do?

Client: I'll look at my notes.

Me: Yes, and, you've forgotten what to say and you are super embarrassed and then you look at your notes…?

Client: I'll look at my notes and I'll start speaking.

Me: Yes, grasshopper, you will.

We didn't stop at the bad part. We figured out a way through to what was next, and next, and next. This envisioning is priceless when girding yourself to do the scary thing. It helps to grow your bravery.

 Don't just imagine your worst-case scenarios. Imagine yourself <u>handling</u> your worst case scenarios by using "what if?" and "what's next?"

Confidence is also derived from *authenticity*. By being your best, truest self, you shine a light that is distinctive and necessary to the world. It's brave to be authentic when the world wants to smooth and box you into someone different.

While working with several women in a public speaking bootcamp, the subject of authenticity came up (as it frequently does when talking about fear, anxiety, and imposter syndrome). While it may seem oxymoronic, authenticity, and a deep understanding of what you bring to the table, is an antidote to these self-limiting ideas and behaviors.

I am not a doctor. Nor am I a psychiatrist or psychologist. What I am is an avid listener and a lifelong student of human interaction. I listen, I watch, I practice, I learn, I teach, and I continue to learn. I know being your best, authentic self is what is required.

In public speaking workshops, people often ask me what gesture they should make, or what movement looks "good." The answer is not a quick or easy one. The answer lives in the moment. "Putting on" a gesture because you saw someone else do it, or adopting a posture that has no root in your "you-ness," is a sure way to let the audience know that you're faking it. It's not organic and it undermines the audience's confidence in you. This ultimately erodes your message.

We have to figure out who you are on stage. Or in the board room. Or at the podium, or wherever you're communicating to two or more people. We have to uncover your presentation persona.

Your presentation persona is not a costume or an alter-ego. It is you. It is the part of you that gets on stage, that communicates with heart and passion, that owns the space and delivers the message. It is you. It's a you that is or has cultivated a very particular set of skills, and has trained to do the thing.

Public speaking is not for the faint of heart. It's audacious. It requires bravery and an imperative. It takes courage to use your voice, regardless of how many people are listening... or aren't.

You didn't come into the world walking and talking and full of knowledge. It was a process. As is developing the range of skills needed to become a really good public speaker. Why would you think that you could just copy someone else's idea of what a "public speaker" looks like and it'll fly?

I've had the privilege to see both Elizabeth Gilbert, author of **Eat, Pray, Love** and Rachel Hollis, author of **Girl, Wash Your Face**, speak at large events. It would not be possible for these women to have more different presentation personas. Elizabeth essentially stood in one spot and told us stories. It was intimate and personal and profoundly lovely. Rachel was loud and energetic and stalked the stage, and we ate it up. Both women connected with their audience. Both understood to whom they were speaking, and both were absolutely brilliant, *because they were themselves.*

So don't ask me about where you should put your hands, and let's stop talking about where you should look at any given moment. Instead, let's work on *why* you want to stand up. Let's figure out your message, your imperative, and your brand. Let's give your audience the best presentation that you can offer, in all of your glorious you-ness. Because no one else can.

6. Speaking on/moderating a panel

Panel discussions are a fantastic way to build your brand and your business identity. They allow people to look at you as a subject matter expert. These panels also give you great public speaking experience that is supported by the other people on the stage with you.

I highly recommend participating in as many panels as you can, and if you're ever asked to moderate a panel, do that too!

Let's talk about being a great moderator, or even a good one. I've seen moderators who monologue'd like they were auditioning for Broadway. I've been a panelist when the moderator was far more interested in sharing her life story than having a conversation with us or the audience. I've also seen really nervous (I guess?) moderators with their stamped-in-concrete list of questions who can only respond to the panelists with a "great, great" or "uh, huh, wow..." before racing to the next question.

So, before we get to panelist guidelines — should you ever be fortunate enough to be asked to moderate a discussion — here are some dos & don'ts:

1. Please, for the love of God, do some research — on the topic, on the panelists.

2. You're the driver, but this isn't your bus. Talk less about yourself and more to the panelists.

3. Understand the audience — to whom are you speaking?

4. Do ask the panelists beforehand for bios and handles (e.g. first names, titles).

5. Don't be afraid to jump into a panelist's response if they're monopolizing the time.

6. Do be respectful if/when you have to curtail a response and move on.

7. Check in with the audience periodically to make sure they're engaged and with you.

8. Ultimately, it's your job to facilitate the conversation, showcase the panelists and make sure the audience walks out having learned something.

Here are my guidelines for being a continually sought-after panelist:

1. Understand the discussion topic and consider your unique perspective — it's why you're there.

2. As always — understanding the audience means knowing to whom you're speaking.

3. Please, please, please, do not give a speech or presentation!Be succinct in your responses — use, as Shakespeare wrote, "… more matter and less art…"

4. When you can, support other panelists and build on their responses.

5. If you disagree with a comment, remain respectful and explain why you disagree with their response — and NOT with them personally.

6. Speak to the audience, not necessarily the moderator.

7. Be your best, most relaxed and engaging self.

BONUS: I-shouldn't-have-to-say-this-but-I'm-gonna-anyway:
No hate speech of any kind. None.

 **For example:**

Scene #1: Ryan was a CFO of a mid-sized landscaping equipment company. He contacted me because he felt that when he spoke at meetings or corporate events, people weren't listening to him and he wasn't making any kind of impact.

What we discovered is that Ryan is a *really* chill guy. Like, really chill. He was monotone and very low energy, so people assumed that he was disengaged. After working together, Ryan was able to find his **public speaking persona**. He shook things up a bit by changing his position in the meeting spaces, he practiced speaking with more energy and less reserve. He developed a more **engaging** speaking style by understanding what his **audience** was looking for from him. Ryan parlayed these new skills into a CEO position with a different company.

Scene #2: Casey ran her own wellness & organization company. We worked together when she booked a speaking gig at a wellness conference and began to freak out about actually speaking.

Over a couple of months, we were able to find the source of her **anxiety** — feeling like she wouldn't have anything new or interesting to speak to this group about. It was imposter syndrome. Casey was able to **rewrite her script** by literally rewriting the script of her talk. We incorporated more of her life— her history, her difficulties and successes, into her program. It became very personal, **authentic** and **imperative**. She told me after the event that she received a wealth of positive feedback and that other participants were incorporating some of her wisdom into their own work.

 **Moving forward:**

Becoming a great public speaker is a process. Public speaking is a linchpin skill that, when honed, up-levels all of your other soft skills.

Growing your public speaking skills is quite frankly, one of the greatest things you can do for yourself.

Start with an honest appraisal of your skills. What exactly scares and excites you about speaking and presenting? What goals do you have in this area? Think about where your skills are now and where you can improve.

1. Look for workplace opportunities to speak — projects, pitches and presentations all offer ways for you to practice and refine your public speaking skills.

2. Watch and listen to other speakers. Find inspiration, not imitation, in the way very successful speakers do what they do. Be specific about what exactly you admire in other speakers.

3. Take a class. Get out of your comfort zone and get into a workshop or a bootcamp that will shake up your status quo. Work with a coach.

NOTE: There are teachers who will suggest that you rehearse in a mirror. I do not. I am heartily against mirror work. We can't effectively assess our skills in mirrors because we cannot separate what we're doing from how we look. It's bad theatre and not at all organic.

Videoing yourself is like mirror work. It's really, really hard to be honest with ourselves about our skills because we're so busy judging our clothes, those extra pounds or any of a thousand other ways we subtract from ourselves. If you want to use video to grow your skills, show the video to someone else. Ask them specific questions about how well you engaged with the "audience," your timing, the quality of your speech and storytelling skills, etc.

Chapter 5

It's Time to "Woman Up"

This conversation is for women and about women.

If you're a guy and have read yourself to this chapter, welcome! Please make yourself at home, listen and continue learning.

I want to talk about being a woman. I want to talk about being a woman now — in the 21st century — with all the perks and problems that come with it. This is a tough love conversation.

You might ask what a "woman talk" is doing smack in the middle of a professional development book about communication and soft skills. It's a good question.

The fact is that we're all a product of everything we've experienced. Every single thing we've seen, tasted, heard and felt is a singular universe specific to ourselves. My perspective and experiences rest with who I am, so the observations that I posit are filtered through my particular lens.

That lens is decidedly female. How I communicate, and how the world communicates with me, cannot be separated from my woman-ness.

Therein lies the rub.

The unfiltered rub is the systemic inequities women face. We know the system is stacked against us because **the system wasn't built for us.**

Our systems of government, education, rules of law, etc. — none of it was built with women in mind. And while we've spent hundreds of years inserting ourselves into systems that would be more comfortable if we weren't there, the progress has been slow and incredibly hard won.

As a White woman, I understand and acknowledge that I move through the world with a privilege that my Black and Brown sisters don't have. The system that wasn't built for us is harsher and more discriminatory for women of color. We know that.

Here's a bit of cold, hard data:

- Women make up the bulk of the workforce but are paid, on average, 18% less than their male counterparts.[2]

- Women are more likely to die by gun violence.[3]

2 Robin Bleiweis. "Quick Facts About the Gender Wage Gap." Center For American Progress. March 24, 2020.https://www.americanprogress.org/issues/women/reports/2020/03/24/482141/quick-facts-gender-wage-gap/

3 Everytown Research & Policy. "Guns and Violence Against Women: America's Uniquely Lethal Intimate Partner Violence Problem." Everytown. October 17, 2019. https://everytownresearch.org/report/guns-and-violence-against-women-americas-uniquely-lethal-intimate-partner-violence-problem/

- While approximately 51% of the U.S. population is women, we make up about 25% of the federal leadership (House & Senate).[4]

- Nearly 1 in 5 women have been raped.[5]

- While women own 40% of the businesses in the US, they receive about 7% of the venture funding for their startups.[6]

This is the tiny tip of the underrepresentation/bias iceberg, and there's an ocean of it. Worth acknowledging is that the statistics are averages, and that if you look deeper into the racial breakdowns, the numbers are worse for women of color on every front.

- Hard, cold statistics are only part of the picture. We experience, we observe, and know:

- 100% of the women I know have been sexually harassed, multiple times.

- 3 out of 4 women in the US have faced sexual abuse, much of it unreported.

- Women are taught early and often that it's their responsibility to "not become a victim," but men are not taught how not to become victimizers.

- 100% of women have been talked over, or "mansplained," furthering the notion that women's voices are not valued.

4 Catalyst.org. "Women in Government: Quick Take." Catalyst: Workplaces That Work For Women. January 20, 2021. https://www.catalyst.org/research/women-in-government/

5 National Sexual Violence Resource Center Summary Report. "Sexual Violence by Any Perpetrator." NSVRC. 2010. Updated 2015, 2018. https://www.nsvrc.org/statistics

6 Maddie Shepard. "Women-Owned Businesses: Statistics and Overview (2021)." Fundera. December 16, 2020. https://www.fundera.com/resources/women-owned-business-statistics

- In the US, women's bodies and reproductive rights are subject to the whims and political leanings of governmental entities. Male bodies are not legislated.

- We know that a disproportionate amount of household duties and child-rearing fall on women, even when both partners work.

- We know that during the COVID-19 pandemic, the bulk of the work/life "restructuring" fell onto women, and we have suffered for it, both mentally and economically. As with everything COVID-19-related, the long-term effects can only be imagined.

- We know that in workplace reviews, men are provided with specific and actionable feedback, while women are offered vague or dead-end criticisms, contributing to an overall lack of women in leadership roles.

- We know that economics plays a huge role in a woman's ability to escape domestic violence, and the chains of generational violence.

- We know that companies that promote women to leadership positions are more profitable.

- We know that historically, the contributions that women have made have been categorically undervalued, co-opted and erased.

When #MeToo hit hard, my female friends and I had many, many conversations about the experiences we've had throughout the course of our lives.

We discussed how, throughout our entire lives and beginning at a very young age, we've had to adopt attitudes and behaviors that the men in our lives did not, as a matter of survival. For example, when I asked my husband if he'd ever done an "I'm alive" date check-in, he had no idea what I was talking about. All my girlfriends, knew exactly what I meant.

I saw a tweet once where the author said that a guy's biggest concerns on a date were how much he was going to pay for dinner and if he was going to get laid, and a woman's biggest concern was not being killed.

It's (not) funny 'cause it's true.

I didn't bring you to this conversation to dwell in the statistics or the anecdotes. We know them. We live them.

If you're a woman, you've lived these truths, and a myriad of others. Queen Beyoncé says girls run the world, but I have my doubts.

If you're a guy, welcome to the party, pal.

The point is this: There is a fundamental disparity between how men and women are valued and treated. We know this because, again, the system wasn't built for us.

To address the disparity, we have to acknowledge the disparity. We can't craft solutions to problems we don't acknowledge exist. For many women, or most women...

Alright, *all* women, that includes the scripts we've been running our entire lives. We're talking about those biases we were trained with that began when we were babies. Our entire society was/is structured around the idea that yes, you can be smart and successful. Yes, you can even be a leader in your field, but the most important thing, the *most* essential thing, the guiding star of womanhood is to be attractive, and fuckable.

Yes, I said the thing out loud.

And, before you shut me down because you think I'm way off the mark, hear me out and consider the following:

Have you ever discounted a woman's abilities because of her appearance? Judged a woman on her femininity or decried her as not "lady-like?" Been "put off" by a woman because she's "too smart?" Dismissed a woman because she's deemed "too aggressive?" How often have you, or your social groups, dissected a woman, particularly a woman with power, based on the sound of her voice, or her hairstyle, or her lipstick color? How many times have you overheard other women tear down a woman, not based her skills or on her failings as a leader, but because she was "too" something. The list goes on and on.

Here's the point — *we women have had a substantial role in upholding systems that don't support us.* It's what we've been taught. It's what we know.

It's time to rewrite our scripts. This is the answer to the question about the reason for this chapter.

By growing our awareness of the way things have been done, we can begin effectively changing how we want to do them in the future. By becoming aware of the inequities that we've supported, we get to rewrite those encounters for the future. We grow our autonomy and build strategic and impactful ripples that change systems.

In **Chapter 3**, we explored coded language. For women, it's all around us. Entire multi-billion dollar industries are built around making sure that women never feel quite *good* enough — that in order to have value, you have to be perfect, and that perfection has little to do with character and everything to do with "beauty."

The problem with this "perfect" is that it's always someone else's unattainable ideal.

Perfection is a marketing strategy, not a human.

Perfection is destructive. Let it go, and embrace the you that you are in this moment. You get to be who you want to be. You get to decide, no matter what came before. This is part of building new systems — holding for ourselves, who we want to be and then giving people the space to adapt to us.

This includes the coded language specifically used on and against us. Language that is designed to degrade us, attack our confidence, and put us in a box. Frequently, the language used *on* women or *about* women is violent. Or leads to violence. Words are a stepping stone to action.

So let's change the words.

As with all coded language, we lessen or remove the power when we reject or "decode" it. Again, we talked about this in **Chapter 3**, and it's big enough to repeat and keep learning.

"You're so bossy!"

After a workshop and during an incredibly robust Q&A, one of the female participants began a question by relating an encounter with a co-worker. Actually, it was a male subordinate, someone that she had supervisory capacity over. She had reminded him of a looming deadline that she was concerned he wasn't going to meet. His bristly response was, "You're so bossy!" Her question was, how do we as women in business, respond to statements like this?

The answer to that question lies in answering a couple of related questions:

    a. Would he have used the word "bossy" to a male supervisor? OF COURSE NOT.

b. What did he *really* mean? He meant, "I'm uncomfortable with you having any kind of effective power over me, though I cannot admit it, so I'm going to REDUCE YOU by using language that is derisive and childish."

Women understand coded language. We've been dealing with it literally forever. We understand that when a "bossy" or "aggressive" is tossed our way, the speaker is attempting to undermine us. We get that when we're referred to as "honey," "babe" or "sweetie" by a male co-worker or the guy ringing us out at the tire repair store, we're being infantilized and put in a box. We get it. They wouldn't use these same words on a male co-worker or a guy they're ringing out at the tire store.

I'm interrupting this rant for a moment to look at the concepts of Miss, Mrs. and Mr. Consider that the word "mister" doesn't declare a marital situation. The guy is simply *mister*. Both miss and missus connote whether a woman is married. Why? Why does our society recognize that a man is a man his whole life, but a woman's life is demarcated by whether she has decided to wed or not? Words matter, my friends. Words matter.

And now, back to our regularly scheduled programming…

Here's how I, and the rest of the participants answered the "bossy" question: **You turn it back around to the speaker.** You ask him, "What do you mean by bossy/aggressive/demanding?" Do you mean someone who is in charge? Do you mean someone who knows what's required to get the job done?"

Again, yes, I know it's a REALLY uncomfortable conversation to have, for both of you, but it's how progress is made. It's how more productive, diverse cultures are crafted. It's what leaders do. We have to have tough conversations well. It's time to stop gritting our teeth and accepting the words that are coded to make us feel small and *less* than.

We can do it one conversation at a time. And, we have to be willing to go against our "training."

We have to be willing to not be thought of as nice. Women are taught from a very young age to be nice, polite, and sweet, or else someone else won't like us. And if someone else doesn't like us, does that mean no man will want to date/marry us?

If we're not nice, how will we ever get a man to take care of us? Who will tell us we're beautiful? How will we be able to have children and a house and a dog?

I don't want to be nice. I want to be good.

I want to be a great business woman. A stellar mother and wife. An excellent friend. "Good" is the value system I create, for me, about me. "Nice" ain't it.

Here's the 21st century truth: You don't have to be anyone's version of yourself.

We're taught that by allowing others to usurp our space/time/efforts, we're doing a good thing, the right thing, and that's just not correct. It's insidious. It's buying into the system that was not built for you. We have to change the system.

One of the ways we change the system is by leaning into being labeled as bold/assertive/aggressive, and by being okay with not being thought of as nice.

Speaking of which, here's a tale of two very different conversations:

I had the opportunity to attend two events in the same week that ended up on opposite ends of the conversational spectrum. One left me feeling empowered, educated, and a little awed. I walked out of the other pissed and exasperated.

The first event was an executive women's luncheon. The attendees were smart, educated and powerful women. Some were C-suite, some were the heads of departments at colleges and universities, and others were running their own companies. The topic of the luncheon was fostering talent development and retention in today's workplace, and the panel was a stellar collection of brilliant females. Hell, the women sitting at my table were 50 shades of amazing. The conversations were smart, funny, and insightful. I walked out of this event having learned from the panelists, connecting to several of the women I knew I would continue to network with and befriending one another. I walked out feeling buoyed and positive.

The second event was an entrepreneurial function. The format for this event is relaxed, open networking while eating a slice of pizza and then settling down to a "fireside chat" with a successful entrepreneur who is questioned about his/her journey. The guest entrepreneur (who we'll call "Bob") was engaging and smart and a pleasure to listen to. He was frank and funny about his education (or lack thereof), his successes and most importantly, his failings. He was thoughtful in his answers and an all-around excellent interview.

After the event ended, I went over to Bob to let him know how much I enjoyed his story, and to ask him a question. Around him were two other men, one was speaking and one was waiting to speak. I smiled and waited, slightly awkwardly, as you do. The first guy to whom he was speaking finally finished, they shook hands (for the fourth time) and the guy walked away. Bob then turned to the second gentleman and began talking. Meanwhile, two other men moved up behind Bob and were waiting to speak with him. When Bob finished with the gentleman he was speaking with, he turned to me. I told him my name, shook his hand and was in the middle of telling him how much I enjoyed his candidness and humor when one of the guys behind him interrupted me and started a conversation with Bob. Bob then physically turned away from me and joined the guy in conversation. I stood there thinking he would apologize and turn back to me, but no... there were men to speak to.

The room was made up of about 75% men and 25% women, which is the ratio of most entrepreneur or start-up related events. I was the only woman who went to speak with Bob and I waited, politely, for about 10 minutes for my turn, only to be "manterrupted." It was systemic. It took collaboration on the part of the men in the circle to exclude me. By turning away, *while I was talking* (I can't stress that enough), and beginning a conversation with someone else, Bob effectively agreed with the man that interrupted me. They, together, decided that what I had to say was less valuable than what he had to say. And that, as they say, is bullshit.

In hindsight, what I could have done is taken a cue from Kamala Harris's playbook and simply said, "I'm speaking" and continued my conversation, but I was "polite."

Human beings sometimes talk over each other. We get excited and passionate and can't stop ourselves from interjecting. This was not that. This was gender biased and dismissive and they probably didn't even realize they did it; *and that is the problem.*

When I left the women's luncheon, I felt empowered. When I left the entrepreneurial event, I was angry. It was not the first or even 100th time that simply because I am a woman, I was discounted. There are a number of studies and articles regarding women being talked over, interrupted and even ignored when speaking. It degrades and limits all of us.

You literally have no idea what you're missing when you ignore half of the conversation. We, all of us, need to work harder to recognize our bias and overcome it. Think collusion and connection, not exclusion. We have to set the table differently in order to feast on all that's available to us.

Part of setting that table is making conscious decisions about what words we'll allow, and what words we won't. I'm a big proponent of thoughtfully chosen words.

If the words we speak are outward manifestations of the words we think, what about the words we ingest over a lifetime? Can you think of words that have been spoken to you or used on you that felt destructive, like weapons? I can.

What you allow, will be.

Stop allowing destructive words into your life, your head. Don't give them a home.

Recently a male business associate left me a voicemail, in which he called me "babe." Normally I would shrug this off. I've shrugged it off a million times before, but this time felt different. Maybe it was his tone or the offhandedness with which he spoke, but I'm actually not his babe, his doll, honey or sweetheart.

Nor am I his girl, lady, chick, baby doll or baby girl. I run a business I'm in the process of making insanely great. I'm a wife and a mother to some incredibly cool people. I am not "babe."

Words matter. In our lives and our businesses, even small words like "babe" matter. These little pebbles of misogynistic throw offs cause damage. He could have chosen to use words like "friend" or "pal," which denote being a peer. He chose not to.

Calling a woman "babe" in a business setting whiffs of subjugation. What might be seen as a term of endearment *isn't* because it doesn't belong there. It's proprietary and inappropriate. We use words to label, box and shelve. The use of terms like "honey" or "sweetheart" for women known casually or in business immediately puts them in a place separate and less than equal to men. As a mother, I struggle constantly to make sure that my daughter doesn't define herself by the small words of others. I don't always win.

Riding this soapbox to the end, let's talk about the word "lady." Since we were children, we've been admonished to act like ladies and/or gentlemen. To me, the word lady, in all its forms, has a very narrow connotation. It speaks of rigid boundaries, properness and conformity. I imagine an older Victorian woman, tightly corseted, drinking tea and looking very, very disapproving.

I am no lady. This Victorian woman I have imagined would agree that I am no lady. I color outside the lines, and I'm bossy and outspoken. I have no desire to be whatever it is *you* think I should be. The responsibility falls on each of us individually to choose our words more carefully, to examine what we are really trying to say. Armed with the knowledge that words have power, we can change the conversations and change the world. Perhaps one small step toward global equality would be to erase "babe" from our vocabulary.

Once, a friend's father described me as a "classy broad." THAT, I am absolutely fine with.

At the end of the day, I want to participate in building new systems. Systems that support and amplify women of all colors and identities.

I want to light candles and amplify voices.

I want to be a person who says, "she's speaking…"

I want to be one of the architects of empowerment for myself and my daughter through word and deed.

I know that we can acknowledge and revel in the differences between us while creating equality and equity for all women. All people.

Together we can build that system.

It's time to do things differently. It begins with small awarenesses, as I said in the beginning. We're creating micro tears in what is in order to become what we want. It is my sincerest hope that by reading this book, you become aware of unprofitable thoughts and habits and you find a doorway to recalibrate yourself to your better, more spectacular self.

How might those small changes create ripples throughout the world?

 **For example:**

I presented a communication workshop geared toward women to a women's legal group. Every participant was an attorney and ranged from a new associate to partner. During the session, we worked on creating strong language choices, recognizing "coded" language and disrupting the habitual in order to create a new normal.

During the event, one woman described how when she was in a meeting with other attorneys, most of whom were male, it's *assumed* that she'll be the one to take notes. Another participant chimed in that she was expected to make the coffee arrangements for her meetings.

We spent a good deal of time workshopping ideas on how to deal with these gender-biased and entrenched roles. One of the solutions we came up with was to state to the group that she would accept the task for this meeting, but the next one is on Bob. Or Carl. Or David.

Another solution was to actively and purposefully say nothing. When faced with the "okay, we need someone to take notes..." and the group looks at the only woman in the room, don't do it. Stay silent. Or, if that seems too difficult, offer to bring in the meeting leader's assistant to handle the note-taking.

Several of the women commented that they are consistently interrupted and/or talked over during these meetings. One of the ways to deal with this is to support each other. If you're in a meeting and a woman is being talked over, interject and let the room know that you wanted to hear from her. Or Wanda. Or Evelyn.

One final bit of advice we discussed for this particular situation was to change the dynamic in the room by standing. Regardless of the informality of the meeting, by standing when speaking, you essentially command everyone to look at and listen to you. You're much more difficult to ignore and talk over when your head is higher than everyone else's. It's strong non-verbal communication.

 Moving forward:

1. Consider the words you use when describing women. Are they descriptive of character and ability, or do they solely describe their appearance? If it is about appearance, what imperative do you have to speak about it?

2. How do you describe yourself? How do you want people to describe you?

3. If you're a woman, can you think of instances where you were ignored, talked over or "mansplained?" How did you deal with it? How could you have dealt with it?

4. Think about an instance where you participated in tearing down another woman. What did you get from that interaction? Affirmation? Bonding?

   Be thoughtful about your motives and consider how you could have gotten whatever it was you received from the interaction, in a different and more constructive way. Be specific with yourself.

5. If you're a man, think of instances where you didn't listen
   or talked over a woman. Why? What would happen if you
   listened better and stopped talking? What about times you
   heard others talking over a woman?

Can you imagine advocating for the person speaking when others talk
over her? What might that conversation sound like?

What words do you use to describe women you like or care about? Are
the words you use about women you don't like centered on appearance
or character?

Chapter 6

Yes, You Have to "NETWORK" Even Though it Sucks and You Hate It

Most of us work, whether at a job for someone else or for ourselves. Or, you're neck deep in the process of looking for work opportunities.

If you're reading this book, chances are you aren't the privileged elite, having been cast high above such gritty realness as having to actually talk to others about what you do and *GASP* listen to them speak about what they do.

Networking has a bad rap. It's seen as a business card grab. A high-pressure sales moment, filled with tight smiles and awkward pauses until someone stares over your shoulder and says, "Oh, is that Paul? I think that's Paul. Will you excuse me? Great meeting you, really." Then they slide by you, sloshing beer on your shoes in a desperate grab for the next great opportunity to sling another card.

Forget that guy and forget Paul.

That is not how good networking is done. And yes, there is a difference between good networking and bad. Stick with me and I'll explain, but first, let's really define networking, shall we?

 Networking is casting a figurative net to create real connections and connectedness with actual people.

Networking is engaging with people to learn if you can create a business relationship of *some kind.*

That doesn't necessarily mean that they're going to buy your widget.

It does mean that they may be a great person to get to know a little better so that you can grow a potential relationship. That relationship *may* include a sale. It *may* include a referral. It *may* include cocktails on the veranda.

Maybe that's just wishful thinking on my part. Who knows?

Here's what I do know…

I have partaken in, and been a victim of, bad networking, and I have learned that there is a better way. In this chapter, we're going to discuss the real world dos and don'ts of networking.

We're going to talk about the fear, the anxiety and the horror.

We're also going to talk about how you can do this thing that you need to do with a certain amount of skill, personality and, dare we say, grace.

Let's start off with the bad news. There are in fact, **three** basic types of networking situations (everything else can be mushed into these three groups):

1. **The "Mixer"** This is the event most people equate to the pleasures of dental surgery. You may imagine having to make small talk, engaging in tedious chit-chat and participating in the ever-present business card grab. You might not be wrong.

2. **The "Networking Group"** This event is designed as an opportunity for all of the people present to make more fulsome connections. It also requires a little something we like to call the "elevator pitch." Cue dramatic music.

3. **The "Opportunity Meet"** This is an unplanned meeting outside of any formal or structured event. It's the door awaiting your knock.

No matter which type of event you're attending, no matter if you meet your ideal customer/boss/partner/mentor in an elevator, at a lunch-time group or at a business cocktail shindig, here's what you always, **ALWAYS** must be prepared with:

a. An authentic and genuine approach to connection;

b. The skill of listening more than you speak;

c. Business cards (duhhh…physical and/or digital, depending on who you're talking with).

Let me break it down for you.

An Authentic and Genuine Approach to Connection

We've already established that networking is necessary. You have to do it, and it's a necessary skill to have to grow any business. So rather than complain, kick and scream about it, here's where you grow skills to *get good at it.* You still may not enjoy networking, but it doesn't have to be actual torture.

Being authentic and genuine means you have to reveal yourself, just a little.

We're talking about being vulnerable enough to be honest with who you are. You want something from the other person/people, right? We're seeking connection and a potential relationship, so it's imperative that you speak about yourself with clear, confident and loving words.

That's right. I said "loving."

The words you use to describe yourself are the words the world will use. Give them the best way to speak about you.

Example:

> **DON'T:** Hey, I'm Ken. I'm a realtor. Are you looking to buy or sell property any time soon?

> • Classic business card grab.

> • The conversation is transactional and impersonal.

> **DO:** Hi there. I'm Ken Smith. My home is my favorite place in the world, so I help others find their favorite places. Where do you call home?

- Full name and a bit of personal information provided.

- Description of work role rather than an actual title or label.

- Includes an invitation to conversation, not a transaction.

Listening More Than You Speak

Active listening is a power skill. It's focusing not only on *what* the person is saying, but *how* they're saying it. It's observing their body language and the emotion with which they're speaking. For networking, it means asking questions and really listening to the answers. This is where gold is found.

 Active listening is one of the best and most profitable skills you can hone to ensure success across the spectrum of your life.

Example:

> **DON'T:** So, nah, not looking to sell? Yeah, I get it. I know West Anytown is nice this time of year. My wife's sister June, we call her Junie B, has a place out there. She's an OB/GYN and makes a bunch of money, so she's sitting pretty.

- Talking too much.

- Offering unwanted information (i.e. relative's nickname and income).

> **DO:** Wow, West Anytown. It's lovely there! What drew you to that particular area?

97

- Open, positive.

- Appropriate reaction.

- Asking a follow-up question that can lead to a real dialogue.

Business Cards

Of course you need business cards! They're a physical representation of you that stays with the person, and hopefully they enhance their recollection of you in a positive way. You always, always need to have a card/cards on you because you never know when you might run into that next stellar connection.

AND, there is a way to offer your card that doesn't make you look like a jerk.

Example:

> **DON'T:** So, I gotta run. Lemme give you my card and if you change your mind about selling, let me know.

- Forcing the other person to take the card.

- Strictly transactional, impersonal and not memorable.

> **DO:** I'd like to continue this conversation, maybe over coffee some time. May I have your card and we can set that up? I'm looking forward to hearing about your crazy move from North Somewheresville. Thank you. It was a pleasure chatting with you and I'll talk to you soon.

- Making the other person feel valued.

- Listening to the what the other person said and reflecting it back to them.

- Asking for their business card (at which point you can offer yours).

- Planning follow-up.

Does this seem difficult? Impossible? WAAYYY past your bedtime?

That's okay. As we said in the beginning, skills are growth items, not put-a-dollar-in-and-get-a-prize items.

The key is to start small.

Plan to attend a mixer, in person or virtually, that's relevant to what you do and/or your industry. Plan to connect with three people. Just three. And, if you've seen the guest list and know who else will be there, you can plan ahead of time which three people you're going to make a point to connect with.

A note about planning: DO IT.

You're going to remove so much stress by planning the things that you are able to plan. This includes working on and practicing your personal introduction. Write it out as a script or as a template that can evolve as you do. Again, find words that are descriptive, accurate and loving to yourself.

Try out your introduction on your partner and friends. Get used to saying the words. And then, get out and actually network!

See, it's not the death monster you imagined.

And once you do the things, you'll find you get better each time and it becomes easier.

Let's shift gears a bit and talk about your **elevator pitch**.

I could write a book about giving a great elevator pitch, (and I will, so be on the lookout), but for now, here's a down and dirty overview.

It's very much like your personal introduction, except that there's a spotlight on you during a pitch. You may have a longer chunk of time in which to make your stellar impression on the crowd.

Aside from clearly and confidently stating your name and work role, the most important part of an elevator pitch is your **value statement**.

Your value statement (AKA value proposition) is the thing that sets you apart in the marketplace. Telling the audience what you do or how do you do a thing better/stronger/faster or with more value than everyone else in the universe.

Your value to the audience, regardless of the size or the situation, is directly linked to how strategically you can communicate what you do, and how well you do it.

I once gave an elevator pitch workshop to a room full of 500 realtors. It was the perfect example of setting yourself apart, even in a room full of people who all did the same type of work. The key was to have each person consider not just what they do as a realtor, but what effect their life experiences, education, work and hobbies brought to the "realtor table."

The realtors at that event walked out with a much greater understanding of how to set themselves apart by being authentic, memorable, and valuable. A good knock-knock joke doesn't hurt either.

Here, for good measure are **five examples of [really] bad networking:**

1. **If you have not allowed the person you're speaking with to actually speak in the last 60-90 seconds, you're not networking, you're delivering a monologue.** Unless your name is Hamlet, quit it! There are few things as frustrating as people who will not shut up about themselves, and who ask you nothing about yourself. I once was "captured" by a chiropractor who spoke for 10 minutes straight and kept a death grip on my arm so I couldn't leave. Keep in mind, it actually isn't all about you.

2. **You dismiss someone after they tell you what they do because it's not useful or interesting to you.** Frankly, this is just rude and belies the actual point of networking, which is to connect and create relationships. While this person's skill set or company may not directly pertain to you, doesn't mean the connection is valueless. Perhaps you know someone to whom you can connect them. Spin the web, baby — it's the whole point.

3. **You spend most of the time at an event standing in a corner, talking to the friend you came with.** *Shaking head sadly* If you have performance anxiety about speaking with strangers, do something about it. Again, spend time rehearsing your introduction or pitch, learn some calming breathing techniques, or register for a class in business communications. Get out of your safe zone and make yourself a little uncomfortable. Networking skills, like all soft skills, are like muscles; you have to actually use them for them to become well defined.

4. **You're there for the free food and booze.** First, the food is generally not very good at these events. And second, the booze is always watered down. If you're not there to meet people and to engage, don't go.

5. **You're only talking to people you already know.** If this is you, you're missing the point completely. It's NETworking. Cast your net, make contact, create connections.

 **For example:**

Scene #1: Years ago when I was first building my business, I was at a "mixer" event for the local chamber of commerce. I randomly introduced myself to a woman who was smiling and laughing with everyone she spoke with. She looked approachable, and since I was new to networking, she seemed like a great person to be one of my three connections for that event (I take my own advice). I introduced myself and listened as Dany told me about herself. She was a copywriter and editor who was going to eventually, begin to work with aspiring authors. We laughed and talked about writing, awkward networking events and perhaps writing the great American novel. We exchanged information and promised to keep in touch.

Months later, I received a call from a mega-giant tech firm inquiring about soft skills training and putting their people on camera. Dany had referred me to them. I got the gig, and have worked consistently for years with the company helping their on-camera people.

Also, Dany has been instrumental in getting this book off the ground. Referrals and connections — you never know what will come of them.

Scene #2: I attended a business women's luncheon where there was to be a panel discussion with executive women from a spectrum of industries. While the food was shockingly delicious, most of the panel participants were lackluster, with one notable exception. Jane, a construction industry marketing/business development person, struck me as smart, funny and definitely someone I wanted to get to know better. At the end of the event, I introduced myself and told her how much I appreciated her candor, and humor, and invited her to coffee some time.

I did follow up with her, and we did have coffee. Over the years, not only has Jane hired me to speak at two different events, but she referred me to an associate to speak at their event. The best part of the story is that, all work aside, she has become one of my best and dearest friends.

Scene #3: Julia had come to me to improve her public speaking skills. In the course of our work, she told me that she was going to be delivering a virtual talk to a diverse group of people on a sensitive subject. After we discussed the gist of what she was going to say, we broke down how she was going to speak about herself and with what words. I encouraged her to speak in a more loving way about herself. We also worked on getting clear about what she wanted to achieve with the group.

She later shared with me that at the end of the talk, the question & answer period was incredibly robust. She had the opportunity to genuinely listen to others in the group. Because she reframed the way she spoke about herself, Julia was sure that others on the call were more open and candid than they might otherwise have been. She has no doubt that she's laid the groundwork for great (net)working relationships.

 Moving forward:

We've established that networking might suck and you may hate it. We've also established that *you need to do it*. Here's how you start building your networking skills:

1. Plan to go to a specific networking event.

2. Write out your personal introduction and elevator pitch script. Practice them alone, with your friends & family and while eating green eggs and ham. Just kidding: No need to bore your family.

3. Plan to connect with three people at the event and then follow up with them in a timely manner.

4. Take stock of yourself after the event and remember our creative studio questions —

   • What worked and is worth repeating?

   • What needs improvement?

Then do it all again, better.

Chapter 7

A Brief Riff on Social Media, Your Phone and the Robot Uprising

This chapter is not about how to get more TikTok® or Instagram® followers.

It's not about how to expand and monetize your YouTube® business.

This chapter IS about future skills, and how best to utilize your soft skills in a social media setting.

As of this writing, more than half of the Earth's population use social media. It's roughly about four billion humans[7]. That's a helluva lot of us.

There's no doubt in my mind that most of you reading this book will be doing so on a tablet or listening to my dulcet tones as you're driving.

7 Global Social Media Stats. "DataReportal." January 25, 2021. https://datareportal.com/social-media-users.

All of this to say, we live in a digital epoch, so you might believe that you don't need any guidance or insight into social media dos or don'ts.

Cool, cool.

Let me just run this by you...

The internet is pretty much forever. As any politician running for office knows, those "deleted" Tweets from five years ago will haunt you in a harsh, harsh way. One of the things most commonly uttered by high school guidance counselors and HR professionals is that anyone recruiting you for a job is going to look closely at your social media accounts. This will only get more profound as time and technology march forward.

What is the conversation your socials are having with the world?

Keep in mind this chapter is 100% NOT about to telling you who to be, particularly on social media.

What I do want to offer is a couple of perspectives on the subject that perhaps you may not have considered:

Each platform has a different audience.

As you know from the chapter on public speaking, in order to speak well to an audience, you have to know what that particular audience wants from you. This is especially true for social media platforms where you have a captured audience.

LinkedIn® wants your most professional and knowledgeable self.

TikTok® is looking for your best dance moves, while Facebook® wants your opinion on the most recent presidential election. And so on.

Deliver *that* you to that particular audience.

It's really okay to keep some things private

Your entire life does not need to be on display on social media.

Social media is a boon to individual opinion. You get to tell the whole world what you think about avocado toast (ewww!), the latest Ryan Reynolds movie (yes, please), and the plight of the red panda (WTH, it's not a panda at all!).

AND, it's important to remember that while social media has become the modern soapbox — sure you can say/show/repeat whatever you like within the platform's guidelines, you don't get to hide behind your screen without consequence for what you're offering up. See afore-mentioned disgraced politician.

Let's be honest. Social media is rarely about dialogue. It is NOT an honest exchange of ideas and views. It is inherently, a passive aggres-sive form of communication. You throw something out into the universe looking for love, or an argument, or confirmation that what we think/feel/believe is valid.

The act of posting, regardless of platform, is an invitation. An "arrive as you are party," if you will. You are literally asking people to like you and stroke your ego and offer commentary that is in agreement with who you are and what you're saying.

It's important to ask yourself, in the middle of the fluffy puppy photos, one important question:

 Is what I'm posting a positive (not perfect) representation of myself to the world?

If this sounds a little high-minded, it isn't. Remember, the internet is forever and someone, somewhere has a screenshot.

Personally, I take a real interest in politics, and communicate about my beliefs on certain platforms. What I don't do, ever, is name-call. No matter how bat-shit bananas some politician's statement might be, or how infuriatingly inaccurate a meme with 2000 shares is, I simply do not. It's a personal standard. If I'm going to write/speak/teach about the toxic effects of name-calling, I have to live it.

Because again, and I can't stress this enough, while you may be free to say what you like, you are accountable for the *consequences* of what you're saying. There are no free passes, even on social media.

There is enough vitriol, harassment and just downright nastiness living on the web. We are a nation of opinions and our Constitution guarantees us the right to express that opinion. However, just because you *can*, doesn't mean you *should*. This may be difficult to believe, but every single idea that forms in our brain doesn't need or deserve to be put on paper or online, and certainly not one loaded down with curse words and name-calling insults. Nor does every post we see that disagrees with our view of the world deserve to be savaged. Scroll on.

The Robots Are Coming

We live in a sparkly, tech-defined era of gadgets, innovations, and unicorns. So much of business is tech, tech-related or tech-ancillary. Which is a really nice way of saying that they're built specifically NOT to include people. It's about thought-less automation. When you utilize an app, you're circumventing any need (or desire?) to interact with other people. And yet...

When you boot up your laptop to handle your Black Friday shopping, you're doing so precisely because you don't want to deal with crowds, lines, cashiers and parking jockeying. In other words, people.

And yet, humans are omnipresent. We imagine and design and build ways to *not* interact with each other, then we're inordinately impressed when someone sends us a handwritten "thank you" note. We're so busy scaling, and swiping, that we forget that what we're building is being built by people, to be used by people to solve a people problem. We're problem-solving our connectedness.

There are apps for that.

Humans are the space in between — we are the creamy center. We are what technology is made of, bounced off and smacked up against. And we're not going anywhere…hopefully. We need other humans. We crave contact and connectedness. We are at our best with each other, and our worst when we hide behind our screens. We do better together.

Statista calculates that there are over 4.5 Million apps on the market between Apple and Android, as of the 3rd quarter of 2020[8], and there are more being built every day. You would think that with all of that technology at our fingertips, our problems would be solved with the push of a button or a swipe of the screen, but we keep finding/making new problems.

Humans are not obsolete. Like it or not, we need each other. We continue to require meaningful interaction with each other. Perhaps, in our matte-shiny, curve-edged, clock-is-ticking digital world, finding ways to connect authentically with each other, whether in our businesses or personal lives, may be our greatest innovation.

8   Statista Research Department. "Number of Apps Available in Leading App Stores." Statista. February 4, 20201. https://www.statista.com/statistics/276623/number-of-apps-available-in-leading-app-stores/. intelligence-more-important

Another Moment for the Robots

I have evangelized the importance of soft skills training for years. I built a business around it. It's what I do. Not to be dramatic, but it's what I live for.

In the early years of my business, talking about soft skills required a lot of introductory education on the definition and practical uses of soft skills. Only then, were we able to move on to more business-related conversations. The term and the importance have now, thankfully, become ubiquitous. The last couple of years, I've seen a decided rise in the number of people evangelizing the soft skill arts, and it's all thanks to the robots.

The robots are coming. In fact, in most manufacturing industries, they've been here already for quite a while. We are an automated society, and will only become more so in the future. Drone deliveries and driver-less cars are a small step. The rise of artificial intelligence means a paradigm shift is coming in how the world works, and how we humans will place ourselves in it.

The rise in AI will provide better and faster medical diagnoses, and more savvy money management decisions as well as a complete restructuring of manufacturing and logistics. What AI won't be able to replicate is relationships. The smart machines can't empathize or inspire humans forward. "It's these human capabilities that will become more and more prized over the next decade. Skills like persuasion, social understanding, and empathy are going to become differentiators as artificial intelligence and machine learning take over our other tasks."[9]

This is why you hone your soft skills.

---

9 Beck, Megan and Libert, Barry. "The Rise of AI Makes Emotional Intelligence More Important."
   Harvard Business Review. February 15, 2017. https://hbr.org/2017/02/the-rise-of-ai-makes-emotional-intelligence-more-important

Dallas Mavericks owner and tech super-guru Mark Cuban believes that the rise of AI will provide new opportunities for liberal arts students. He was once quoted as saying, "I personally think there's going to be a greater demand in 10 years for liberal arts majors than there were for programming majors and maybe even engineering," he said. "When the data is all being spit out for you, options are being spit out for you, you need a different perspective in order to have a different view of the data."[10]

Creative people, empathetic people and people who can connect with other people are the people of the future.

It is incumbent on us to look at and to look past the next couple of years to understand how our job market is evolving. We need to start thinking right now how we're going to prepare ourselves with not just the technical skills needed to get a job, but with the human skills that will allow each of us to compete in widely changing job markets for the rest of our lives.

Thank goodness you bought this book.

Also, there's the whole "…Terminator/gotta take down Skynet," thing…

We Still Have to Talk About Your Phone

I LOVE teaching people about non-verbal communication. It opens vistas of understanding about the conversations we're having that we didn't *know* we were having.

One of my favorite parts of those sessions is when we talk about the physical "things" that we purposely put in front of ourselves. When

10 Morad, Renee. "Why Mark Cuban Believes Liberal Arts is the Future of Jobs." Forbes. February 28, 2017. https://www.forbes.com/sites/reneemorad/2017/02/28/why-mark-cuban-believes-liberal-arts-is-the-future-of-jobs/?sh=6972fe177a92

public speaking, people like to stand behind a podium or table or their notes, as if those things were Dumbo's magic feather. Some of it is necessary — you need a place to put down your notes. Utility aside, we will purposefully look to put things between ourselves and our audience so that we can mask or soothe our public speaking anxiety.

At networking events — where people are seated, and then stand to introduce themselves — they'll frequently circle around the back of their chair and hold on to it like it was driftwood off the Titanic. These actions are a non-verbal conversation with the audience, that these *things* are more important than you, the speaker. When you stand behind a chair, you've placed a figurative wall between you and the audience. It might make you *feel* less vulnerable, but it *looks* like you're not confident or that you're afraid of actually connecting with us.

And then there are our phones. The small device that fits in the palm of our hands can create a chasm of space between us. The act of placing our phones on a table or desk in front of us is a non-verbal conversation that goes something like this: "Sure, I'm talking to you and I'm probably going to pay attention to some of what you're saying, that is until something better posts/pops/dings or rings." It's frankly, a shitty way to engage with someone.

We've entered a codependent relationship with metal, silicon and plastic.

We've created our own personal "Mean Girl."

She wants all the attention.

All. Of. It.

Sure, you might look at live people, you might even talk to live people, but woe to you if you miss an opportunity to "like" your friend's Insta post about her redonkulous new shoes. Or a semi-important email. Or a tagged LinkedIn® post. Or your cousin's photo of her son's first day of 4th grade.

We're never offline and it's exhausting!

Your phone needs to constantly be reassured that it's the most important thing in your life. After all, you've put your life in your phone. It wakes you up, keeps your calendar, entertains, informs and educates you. You know your place in the world because of your phone. It's your "friend," your lifeline — it just doesn't make you coffee. Mean girls never do, although, there are plenty of apps for that.

And how much time during the day do you spend charging your phone, thinking about charging your phone, or worrying that you don't have enough charge to get you through until the next outlet? Mean Girls are demanding. They want what they want, when they want it.

We haven't even talked about status. You know that boost you get from walking around with a brand new, latest model of whatever phone you have a relationship with. It's exciting and costly and sure, it might be a bit shallow but it's so pretty and you just want to show it off.

You spend huge amounts of time with your phone. Maybe it isn't your friend, but your "frenemy." You know you need some time apart, and that the relationship isn't entirely healthy. You've read the studies. You watched the Simon Sinek video[11]. And yet, the vaguely blue light is a siren call. It's lovely and irresistible, and validating.

Just please, stop trying to make "fetch" happen.

 You have the right NOT to be available 24/7/365.

11 Sinek, Simon. "SAI: Questions & Answers With Simon Sinek - How Do Cell Phones Impact Our Relationships." School Administrators of Iowa YouTube. September 2, 2015. https://www.youtube.com/watch?v=R0xYCy2eft8&feature=youtu.be

Moving forward:

Yes, this was a short, tough-love conversation on the technology components threaded through our lives.

Social media, your phone as an integral part of your life, and the AI that inhabits it are not going away. We humans have to do an excellent job of human-ing, even when we're not face-to-face.

1. Be mindful of how you treat the people you can't see.

2. Protect your peace by taking breaks from socials.

3. If given the choice, always choose an in-person, face-to-face conversation. **Always**.

Chapter 8

You Are Not for Everybody — Embracing Your Uniqueness

Years ago, when I began to contemplate the idea for my distinctive business, I thought *everybody*, everybody would love and appreciate what I had to offer. After all, who couldn't stand to improve their communication/soft skills, and who wouldn't want to do it in a fun and interactive setting? In my enthusiasm, I forgot one of the basic tenets of auditioning as an actor:

I am not for everybody.

I had forgotten that regardless of how brilliant, beautiful and talented an actor might be, there are a million different reasons they don't get the job that have *absolutely nothing to do with them*. Whatever you put into the world, whether it's art, an app, an end table, a training business or yourself, it is not for everyone. Not everyone will want, need, desire or even be interested in what you're offering.

And that's okay.

One of the most influential business books I've ever read is Seth Godin's *Purple Cow*. In it, he expounds on the idea that conformity cannot equal maverick-ism and that you must revel in what sets you apart. Says Mr. Godin, *"The real growth comes with products that annoy, offend, don't appeal, are too expensive, too cheap, too heavy, too complicated, too simple — too something (of course, they're too 'too' for some people, but just perfect for others)."*[12]

When I started my business, I had to spend a lot of time educating people on the value of soft skills before I could educate them on the value of my business. We further set ourselves apart by utilizing theatre strategies as the platform for what we do. It's scary to some people. It's different and unusual, and I was repeatedly told by people I respected that I should take theatre completely out of the equation. I opted not to listen to them. I believe, as Mr. Godin eloquently writes, *"In your career, even more than for a brand, being safe is risky. The path to lifetime job security is to be remarkable."*

Some people will not like you. Perhaps you're too loud, too quiet, too smart, too funny or too tall.

Some people will not see your value. That's okay because…

You are not for everybody, and everybody is not for you.

---

12 Godin, Seth. Purple Cow: Transform Your Business by Being Remarkable. 2009. Portfolio, a Member of Penguin Group (USA) Inc.

And that is as it should be.

A moment of clarity — your value to someone else has nothing to do with your humanity. Your worth as a human is never in question.

You don't have to ingest every negative comment, every side-eyed look, every failed endeavor, every moment that didn't go your way or exactly as planned, as proof that you are somehow less-than. "Embrace the suck," as Facebook COO, Sheryl Sandberg, wrote, and move on.

For the next little while, we're going to talk about and unpack the idea of uniqueness. This chapter isn't necessarily about growing new skills, but standing with confidence in who you are in this moment, and embracing the journey.

Who you are, and how you do what you do — whether it's parenting, your work, or your art — is unequaled in the universe, since not one other person has your combination of skills, abilities and experiences. You are a unicorn. It's your you-ness that is your superpower.

This entire book is about how to wield and hone that superpower. This chapter is about recognizing and embracing it.

Let's Begin With Perspective

This is your view of the world. Perspective is made up of your experiences and background, which helped form your thoughts and ideas about the world in which you live.

Perhaps you've heard of the juggernaut Broadway musical, *Hamilton*. If, unlike me, you are not a theatre geek, let me give you the lowdown…

Author Ron Chernow wrote an exhaustive biography of Founding Father, Alexander Hamilton in 2004. As legend now has it, writer/

composer Lin-Manuel Miranda, while on vacation in Mexico in 2008, began to read the book and was inspired to write *Hamilton*, the musical. In Alexander Hamilton, Miranda found an immigrant of "low" birth, who was drawn to the power of written words, and desperate to help shape a nation that was "young, scrappy and hungry." In the stage production, he brought to life a world where culture, race, ego and economics collide in congressional rap battles overflowing with smart, cutting rhymes and anthemic beats.

The show garnered oceans of praise, the likes of which haven't been seen on The Great White Way in decades. The production set a record for the number of Tony Award nominations and awards it received. It won a Grammy, and Mr. Miranda was awarded the Pulitzer Prize in Drama. The show, as they say, has legs.

Here's why any of this should matter to you: Miranda took a subject as seemingly dry as 11th grade American history and dramatically changed our perspective on it. With a production that contains music as diverse as rap & hip hop, to 60s British pop and Broadway standards, he didn't let what has *always been done determine what he will do*. The show is provocative, not only because of the content and the format, but also because of its non-traditional cast. None of the Founding Fathers portrayed in the show are white, and it works because the show is that good. It is fresh, smart and innovative.

Mr. Miranda is the son of immigrants. That Alexander Hamilton was also an immigrant, resonated with him. He related to that perspective.

Musicals don't usually make big money. It's a sad fact of Broadway lore, but this one does. A *lot* of money. Unicorn-level money. The show is so successful Miranda has created an educational platform in which local high school students can see the production for free, and have an opportunity to interact with the cast. That kind of impact is profound and far-reaching. Lin-Manuel has taken his skills, his passion and his interests and created something that shouldn't theoretically work. It does though, and he's built an empire on it.

Your perspective is singularly unique, which is why, in **Chapter 9: Another Riff: Empathy and Why Everything is Not Always About You**, we stress the importance of looking at life from someone else's perspective. If our perspective is tunnel vision, then empathy is a variety of lights in the tunnel.

In 2012, my family and I moved from Upstate New York, to Charleston, South Carolina. It was a giant move in a lot of ways, not just the geographic 1000+/- miles.

1,000 miles can make a very large difference in perspective. For one, it's hotter in Charleston, and not just a bit hotter, but a LOT. In the time we've lived here, I have donated most of my heavy sweater collection. Big sweaters are about as outmoded as knit scarves. I am still astounded that I can make it through the depths of winter with only a sweatshirt. The sun feels closer. I suppose it is since we're 1,000 miles closer to the Equator. This change in latitude has crystallized the concept of perspective for me. The people here are different from people in New York. I suppose they would have to be, given that they are used to living in a roasting pan.

Life here is a tad slower. Again, maybe it goes back to the heat. "No need to rush, we're all going to get there but let's do it without heatstroke and by-the-way, let's have some sweet tea," is pretty much the subtext to every conversation. The change in perspective is awesome. In Upstate New York, you only have a few months of really lovely, warm weather before you have to literally gear up for winter. Here, the entire transition consists of going from flip-flops to close-toed shoes and back again.

I so appreciate this change in perspective. It has given me another view of life, and is now a part of my history and my superhero backstory.

You Are a Disco Ball

When I was growing up, my parents frequently told me that I was "too sensitive," "too emotional" and "too dramatic." My sisters both told me that I was "too bossy" — I'm the oldest. Early boyfriends let me know that I was "too picky" or "too demanding." My teachers told me that I was "too quiet" and "too talkative," and that I read too much (true story!). It seemed that I was somehow always "too much," and "not enough" at any given moment.

I know now this story is commonplace. It's a human quality to identify and "box" other people, so we know how to understand and interact with them.

We humans love our boxes. Perhaps because we need to see the world in absolutes in order to make sense of it and deal with it. We label, categorize, and file everything so that we can decide to engage, how to engage, or dismiss completely. This, of course, includes other humans. The problem is that humans are fundamentally "unboxable."

We're in a rush. We gather our information, regardless of how incomplete it may be, at top speed. We live in a swipe left or right era of snap judgments about everything, especially people. The quicker we can weigh and measure a concept, idea or a person, the quicker we can move on to the next thing that needs to be weighed and measured. And so on and so on, but what are we rushing to? The completion of a "to-do" list? The next meeting? The next bingeable series?

In our rush to move quicker, to execute faster, to categorize and dismiss, we are missing big things. Things like color, texture and profundity. People are rarely, if ever, a "this or that" proposition. We're too much. We are both "basic" and "extra" at the same time. We are emotional and situational and irrational and ridiculously, breathtakingly amazing. We have good and bad days and total shit days. How dare we attempt to put the all of any human's existence in a box and label it?

Here's my theory of people: humans are giant disco balls.

Yes, you read that correctly. You are a disco ball.

Disco balls are covered with hundreds of little mirrored pieces of glass that reflect the light, wherever the light finds it. You can't see the entirety of the ball at one time — you constantly have to shift perspective to see different facets. That's human. We are never just one thing at any time. Disco balls aren't static. To function and do its job, a disco ball is constantly turning, changing, absorbing and reflecting. The same thing goes for humans.

You must be willing to spend time, to shift perspective to get the full picture. Photos of disco balls don't do it justice because they're two-dimensional. Humans, like disco balls, are multi-dimensional. We require light and time and space to unveil ourselves.

I was once asked to speak at a conference about leading as an introvert. The more I thought about it, the more I realized that "introvert" is part of a larger filing system. It's just a word used to box and categorize people. We don't have to live in the box. We can live outside, above and below any box we choose. It only takes a little more time and a slight bit of effort to recognize how non-categorical, how unboxable, we each are.

You get to decide what particular stardust you offer to the world. The world does not get to decide that for you.

Peoples is Peoples

If you haven't surmised yet, this chapter is a screaming cheer in praise of individuality. In praise of *your* individuality. The quirks, faults, ambitions, talents, and heart that is you, is what the world requires. We are designed to be different from each other. And while it's important to find our tribes and people we can communicate and connect with, it's our differences that are beautiful and textural. If you can only see the color purple, then there is no such thing as purple.

Our Humanity is Our Commonality.

Many years ago, there was a scene in a Muppet® movie that has stuck with me as an equalizing touchstone. Before you disdain a singing bunch of questionably coiffed puppets, remember that there were a lot of humorous life lessons to be learned (including tolerance for inter-species romances) from them.

In this particular moment, Kermit The Frog® asked a restaurant owner for some advice, and this was his response:

"Peoples is peoples. Peoples eat spaghetti, spaghetti has meatballs. Peoples is peoples."

It may seem like nonsense, but upon further reflection, I don't think so. I think it's a succinct way of acknowledging our humanity — the commonality underlying the universe of differences between us. The fact that this bit of cosmic reflection is propagated by a human-like construction of felt, fabric, and wires only adds to the richness of the observation.

 **For example:**

I'm participating in a virtual business summit and there is a panel discussion on "branding," which is another one of those catch-all phrases that describe a lot of ideas stuffed into one hat. I believe branding to be the totality of how you present yourself to the world. Whether you're a gigantic conglomerate, a solo entrepreneur, or an employee, branding is how you give who you are and what you do to the world.

During this panel discussion, there were four speakers who could not have been more diverse in their ethnicity, gender, age and field of expertise. One was a manager in a large corporation, two were entrepreneurs and one had just accepted a new position. Each one, without exception, embraced authenticity and being true to who they were as part of their path to success. They understood that *no one else can do what they do, in the way they do it.*

The world requires *you.*

 ## Moving forward:

Embrace your you-ness by creating an "**I AM…**" list. This is an ever-evolving, growing, and fluid list of your skills, abilities, talents and proclivities.

My list looks a little like this:

I AM a fantastic writer.

I AM an excellent mama.

I AM a detailed organizer.

I AM a good cook.

I AM a mediocre singer.

I AM breathing and alive.

Acknowledge the great and the not-so-great, the brilliance and the buffoonery. Embrace the you that you are *in this moment.*

Keep this list. Add to it over time, and be gentle with yourself. You deserve it.

Chapter 9

Another Riff: Empathy and Why Everything is Not Always About You

Here's something you may or may not already know: The world does not revolve around you.

I know, I know.

But, before you slam the book closed with an eye roll and a grunt of frustration at such a pedestrian platitude, stop and really consider this idea.

We move through our lives living in our own heads. Everything we see, experience, learn or interact with is run up the flagpole that is us. We are the center of our own lives. Everyone is the center of their own lives.

The world does not revolve around you. *Your* world revolves around you.

Because we exist with other people — and their universes intersect and overlap with our own — empathy is a key human skill. In fact, I believe it's one of the most important soft skills to consider, hone and implement. Empathy is the human trait that is most often referred to when considering what people with antisocial personalities lack.

Hence, its own chapter.

Let's start at a definition. Many people confuse sympathy with empathy believing they're interchangeable. While similar, they are different and the difference is the where the good stuff lives.

Sympathy is sharing feelings for another person. There is a space between us, as in "that's sad."

Empathy is sharing feelings as if they were your own. I imagine what you're feeling and feel that myself, as in "I feel sad too."

Can you "grow" empathy? Can you exercise it like it was your bicep or glutes and make it stronger, or is it a "born with it" kind of skill?

The answer, like most things, lies in the middle. We're probably born with a capacity for empathy *and* it must be fostered as we grow and mature.

I believe we can train ourselves to look outside ourselves and create this emotional connection with other human beings.

 Connectedness is the crux of empathy.

When my daughter was growing up, one of the questions we would ask her when faced with her negative behavior towards another child was "how would you feel if that happened to you?" In our conversations, we would talk about those feelings, and how to address those situations while honoring herself and others.

One of the most important doorways to empathy is the omnipresent question, "what if…?" Look at the people around you, the people with whom you work or live. Your lives may intersect, you may share a life, but you can't share their life unless you're willing to ask yourself "what if that was me?" It requires work and thoughtfulness.

It requires that you thoughtfully consider not only your actions and your "whys," but other people's motives as well. Examining ourselves is work, but as Socrates said, "the unexamined life is not worth living." No person lives in a vacuum, operating independently of their thoughts and feelings. We're all driven by the emotional life we carry inside of us. Other people only get to see the external manifestation of that life.

Think about all of the cop shows and movies you may have seen — how tremendously important is motive to solving the crime? We seek to understand the *why* of it.

At this point, you may be asking yourself, "what's in it for you?"

Why put in the work and the effort to become a more empathetic person? What will that get you?

As it turns out, a lot.

Empathy is a strong leadership skill. When you can imagine the effects of hiring/firing/policy decisions on your workforce, you can make more strategic and profitable decisions. This is a central theme of creating excellent workplace culture, which makes the venture more profitable overall.

Growing your empathy skills will positively affect ALL of your relationships. Every. Single. One.

By thoughtfully considering the actions and circumstances of another person, we can find connectedness to our own actions and circumstances. They may not be identical, but provide us with enough of a bridge that we can create empathy. To imagine that it's YOU in that situation and to imagine what you might do, what you might think and how you might feel. To take that examination, use it, and move forward. That is empathy.

When our spouse or partner comes home from a long day at work, where nothing seemed to go right and traffic was miserable, it's easy to empathize. We know what that's like because we've been there. We've experienced mistakes and failures. We understand profound frustration.

My friend is going through a heartbreaking divorce. It's not necessary for me to have gone through a divorce to imagine what she might be feeling. I feel her grief and bewilderment at the loss of her marriage, and her resolution to build her life again. I can feel with her because I can imagine the ways that this catastrophic loss hits her heart.

It's easier for some people than others. Some folks have a harder time finding the bridge.

That's where the work lies.

I believe we all want love and acceptance, in whatever forms we can find it. We want to belong. We want to be seen and heard. This is the foundation of empathy — letting judgement fall away and creating connection.

I recently had the opportunity to re-watch an episode of CNBC's *The Profit*. For those of you not familiar, CEO Marcus Lemonis goes into struggling businesses and offers advice, mentorship and potentially an investment to the leaders of the business, in the hopes of creating an extremely lucrative endeavor.

In this episode of the show, the business owner had completely alienated himself from his employees. He found fault with everything they did, and saw them as nothing more than tools. During a confrontational moment, when the business owner was faced with Mr. Lemonis, a number of employees AND a workplace psychologist explaining to him that the employees were desperately unhappy, he refused to listen. All he did was insist that he was a good boss, and that it was everyone else that had the problem. His solutions to the difficulties they were facing were to fire everyone and hire new employees. This man simply would not accept that there was any common ground between himself and his employees. He wouldn't listen and certainly didn't speak to anyone in a way that showed he valued them. He subsequently lost a very lucrative opportunity.

How can we find commonality with someone who we seemingly have nothing in common? The answer, of course, is empathy. The business owner in this television show did not have the skills or the desire necessary to understand, or even listen to, the needs of his employees. He was incapable of empathy and so, unfortunately, he and everyone around him lost in a huge way.

 Empathy requires intent. You must want to build a connection.

 **For example:**

Scene #1: My company and I have crafted a "perspective" workshop that is incredibly experiential and sensory driven. Toward the end of the program, participants build literal table-top bridges utilizing a variety of un-bridge-like materials (e.g. pipe cleaners, marbles, wooden stars, feathers, etc.). We ask them to choose their favorite 5-6 (out of 14-15) items *before* we tell them what they are going to do with them. Then, as part of the exercise, we ask them to **build a bridge**, and describe their bridges to the group, explaining their choice of materials and the thought processes behind the build.

What we discovered in the course of producing this event repeatedly, is that people often chose items that had meaning to them — the way something felt when they touched it, or a memory it conjured. Because of that, the bridges they built were personal and powerful.

We then ask them to trade seats with others at their table so they can literally change perspective and view someone else's bridge from their point of view. The emotional responses and discussions stemming from the participants is rich and vast. Everyone involved says that the exercise is provocative and enlightening from a **creative play** and empathy perspective. Several managers reached out for more ways to incorporate play and empathy into their workplace cultures.

Scene #2: A consulting client, we'll call Tom, is an executive with a small equipment company. He was finding that he was not getting the most positive results from his interactions with his team members. When we dove into various situations, he explained that he would frequently walk up to his team member's cubicles and start speaking. We discovered that there were some potential negative **non-verbal conversations** happening — him standing over the person who is seated, and him "barging" into someone's space. We made these discoveries by utilizing **role-reversal strategies**, and then asking how it feels to have someone in a more powerful position stand over you, and how that might feel if it's unexpected.

By putting himself in their shoes, he was able to gain empathy and more profitably interact with his team. He changed how he approached the person's cubicle and began his conversations by asking a "social lubrication" question like, "how was your weekend?" or "have you tried the new deli?" and really listening to the answers before moving to his original purpose.

 **Moving forward:**

Start by being very deliberate in thinking about who and why you want to create connectedness. In what areas/relationships do you believe that you're weakest? Strongest?

If you lead a team, how can you utilize empathy skills to help that team become more cohesive and bonded? Keep in mind that "team" is a flexible word. It can mean workplace manager or project leader, and it can also mean family, a friend group, or your pop-up dodgeball game pals.

1. Work on your "emotional intelligence," or EQ. Recognize and label your own emotions and understand how those emotions drive your thinking and actions. We rarely have single emotions — anger is often mixed with fear. Joy is frequently the baby cousin to pride and relief. The greater skill you have at recognizing the cues in yourself, the better you'll be at recognizing those in others.

2. Value your (personal) social networks and express that value.

3. Grow your empathy skills by putting yourself in their shoes. Imagine what it feels like to be that person, in that situation, at that time and place.

Be curious about other people.

Chapter 10

Squad Goals — Being a Stellar Part of the Team

People are hard.

Living with people is hard.

Working with people is hard.

Let's face it, other people are sometimes the worst. Not us though, we're never the worst.

I'm always smiling, pleasant, open to ideas and ready to pitch in, whatever the situation. Sure I am.

Okay, I'm lying.

People are hard and sometimes our days are full of coping with people who rate high on the jerk-meter. It's all so difficult, *and* we need each other to survive. Human bonds were built and evolved based on our social connectedness.

We work together, live together, build communities, cities and states together. We've constructed rules and laws that help us create existence and thrive together. We require each other. You're never *not* going to interact with other people, or not be dependent on someone else — unless you decide to chuck it all and live off the land in southern Jungleitzistan. In which case, pack plenty of clean underwear and bug spray.

Welcome to the world of teams! In this chapter, I'm going to share with you our Big Four Squad Goals for stellar teaming.

Being part of a team, whatever type of team it is — work, family, community, etc. — is inevitable. Being a valuable, contributing member of that team requires a look at your skills. Together we'll look at some of the most valuable skills when team building.

But First, a Little Perspective

Some time back, my daughter and I were looking for a family-friendly show. We decided to step outside of what we might normally choose and landed on *The Great British Baking Show*. Each episode is built around three ridiculously difficult baking challenges the contestants must ace in order to become Britain's Best Baker. The judges are Mary Berry (yes, her real name) and Paul Hollywood (yes, his real name), the good cop/bad cop of the baking world.

I have no idea what the contestants go through to be on the show. I imagine it must be pretty stringent. I imagine they have to prove that they have more than some basic baking skills in order to get a place on the show. I envision flour flying, butter whipping and tears flowing in front of closed oven doors, which is actually much of what happens on the show.

What I've learned watching the show is that ingredients play differently depending on how they're combined. Certain types of flour react to specific rising agents. Flavors you never thought would go together are shockingly delicious, and butter is necessary in pretty much everything.

In a particularly sticky episode, the task was to bake a cookie. This was to be a "signature" item — one of the baker's own recipes. The cookie crumbled when one of the contestants, we'll call him "Bob," inadvertently used salt where sugar was required. When Paul Hollywood took a bite, he knew instantly what happened and said that it "… failed as a cookie." I began to think a lot about that comment, particularly in the context of teamwork.

Cookies, like organizations, are created and sustained around individual components coming together to create a whole that is more than the sum of its parts. It's that whole that is the purpose and function of the organization. Or, in this case, the cookie. If you make a cookie that is not edible, then you haven't actually made a cookie. You've made a delicious looking paperweight, *and that's not the purpose of a cookie.*

Organizations are built on teams, which are composed of individuals. If those individuals are not executing the goals of the team, then the organization itself is not functioning to its purpose. That's why creating cohesive, productive teams is imperative to the success of any organization. Granted, humans are not sugar and spice, so there are bound to be personality conflicts and style issues. The key is to find individuals and build teams whose flavors compliment and complete each other and set aside the ingredients (individuals) that don't work in this particular mix. These are the teams that are successful, and in turn, make the organization successful. These are the teams that fulfill the purpose of an organization.

135

There may well be a market for cookie-shaped paperweights. There may even be a segment of the population that wants to eat salt cookies, but I can tell you that Bob did not win the title of Britain's Best Baker. Bob got kicked off the show that week.

Squad Goals Skill #1 — Create Shared Goals

A team, by definition, is a group of people with a shared goal.

Imagine a crew of people rowing a boat. There's no sail or motor on board. The only power they have to move is each other.

Imagine that the folks on the port side of the boat are furiously rowing in an attempt to reach an island. Also imagine that the folks on the starboard side of the boat are vigorously rowing in the opposite direction to reach an island off their side of the boat.

No one is going anywhere.

All the action, the energy, the maniacal rowing is for naught, since everyone is working against each other. All the boaters have different goals, and because of that, so much time, energy and talent is wasted.

It's a trite trope that we have to work together. Whatever our team looks like, wherever we're teaming, nothing can be accomplished if we don't work together.

Shared goals are *storytelling*. We are imagining together a future that doesn't exist. We're sharing the narrative of what we would like to be, where'd we like to go and how we'd like to get there. If each person on the team is working with a different story, then we're not sharing goals and we're not existing as a team.

As an actor, I once worked with a playwright who was so guarded about his script that he would only give us a few pages at a time as we rehearsed. It was a nightmare. We were so lost without the full story. We couldn't build our characters or craft relationships because we were missing vital information. We weren't able to understand the journey, and it didn't take long before it all sadly and angrily fell apart. The show never opened.

 If we're not all working together to get to the same place, we're only a collection of people.

In order to have a shared goal, we have to communicate the story of that goal with each other. We must be willing to discuss our direction, our vision, our personal goals, and our beliefs.

We have to understand what, uniquely, each of us brings to the table. To use the cookie analogy, chocolate chips can't do the job of baking soda, and eggs don't function like flour. Each member of a team has to be valued for what they contribute.

Of course, people are not chocolate chips, and there may be overlaps in actual people's skills. Brilliant! Lucky you!

BUT, if, as a team, you're not utilizing the highest and best use of each person skills to get to an agreed upon goal, or goals, then you're not actually teaming well.

Everything is communication, so your goals — the big ones and the tiny ones — must be transparent and understood by the entire team. We all need to know where we're going so we can row in the same direction. Consider using specific "formulas" to develop shared goals, like SMART (specific, measurable, achievable, realistic & time-limited) or OKR (objectives & key results).

Squad Goals Skill #2 — Communicate in an Agreed Fashion

Remember in the beginning of the chapter on communication we said communication is information transferred within "… a common system of symbols, signs, or behavior?"

Yep. Still true. Still necessary, *especially* where teams are concerned.

If you're sending me messages via a particular app, and I'm looking for SMS messages on my phone, we're missing each other.

If our team agrees that we're going to report our progress to management at a specific date and time, and half the team doesn't show up for the call, that's unsuccessful teaming AND really poor communication.

If, though we've previously agreed to take turns speaking, and we're actually just shouting over each other, then we're not fulfilling our agreed upon behavior, and we aren't teaming well at all.

 Plan for good communication.

Have a conversation about how you'll have conversations.

Once your team understands your shared goals, discuss how information will be transmitted, by whom, and when. The communication plan is part of your goal storytelling. Make sure that everyone on your team understands the logistics and timing.

Squad Goals Skill #3 — Listen Like You Mean It

Repeating again what we learned in the communication chapter, listening is so much more than *hearing* what someone said.

Listening actively is about opening up your view of the person and situation so that you can hear not only the words they're saying, but so you can understand the emotion they're speaking with and what their body language is telling you.

You listen for information and meaning.

Think of it as a portrait puzzle. Listening to only the words is a small piece and cannot give you a full picture of the person.

Remember when someone was upset, and you asked them if they were okay and they responded with "I'm fine?" The words are telling you that nothing's wrong, but their energy told you that they were upset. You saw the emotion on their face, the way they were holding their body and how they were behaving. You understood that the words contrasted with the actual meaning.

 Hearing is passive. Listening is active and participatory.

Squad Goals Skill #4 — Make Space for Conflict

We know it's going to happen. We've already established that people are hard, and no group of people can ever agree on anything all of the time. It's impossible. It's inhuman.

Shit will happen. Shit will go down. Shit will hit the fan.

You know that, so let's use that knowledge.

 Conflict is not inherently bad.

Disagreement can be a path to growth. It's where ideas are born and where weaknesses in our plans and ideas are discovered. We'll dive a little deeper into it in **Chapter 11: Conflict Is Scary And *Mostly* Necessary.**

For now, when we're thinking specifically about our teams, we need to plan for disagreement.

It's a heck of a concept, right?

Planning for conflict sets out a roadmap of how we'll handle the inevitable clash of ideas, behaviors and intentions. It must be part of our conversations about goals and communications. It also gives us the opportunity to prepare while we're calm and cool, about a time when we may be upset, disgruntled, or feeling unheard.

Making space for conflict sets the table for spectacular teaming. By, as a team, acknowledging upfront (remember, conversations about how we have conversations…), that conflict is natural and disagreeing with each other will happen, we can decide the process of overcoming those conflicts.

Decide, up front, that conflicts will be discussed. Out loud. This isn't to put anyone on the spot or hot seat, but more to indicate that there are open lines of communication. One way to do this is to save a space in meetings for "Discord & Harmony" moments where there is a limited amount of time set aside to talk about and resolve issues. Again, read and re-read the chapter on conflict for more insight on how to have those conversations.

In the walnut chocolate chip cookie delight that is your team, no team member is more important than any other. It's the collective that makes a cookie, and it's how well they connect and interact each other that makes a spectacular cookie.

I mean spectacular team.

📣 **For example:**

Scene #1: My client, June, had built a team of individual contractors to work on a small government project. Every person on her team was also part of other organizations, so it was important that she communicate the processes they were going to undertake in furtherance of the project goals. She dropped the ball a bit, and ran into difficulty when she discovered that her team members were unclear in how they were supposed to provide their pieces of the project. Also, there were questions about who was doing what exactly, since there was some overlap in skills.

I helped June resolve the issues by setting up communication guidelines for the team — how *frequently* they would communicate, how they would communicate (via a specific app and not a conglomeration of texts, calls, emails and homing pigeons), and really delineating tasks. The final piece was creating a specific space and time for the team, via virtual chat, that they would come together to speak specifically about difficulties and what needed improvement. The team was able to problem-solve together, and June was able to track the problems raised in those conversations, ensuring that those specific issues were resolved and not repeated.

June and her team so successfully completed that project that they were asked to handle a similar undertaking for a neighboring city.

Scene #2: I was running a team-building event at a large travel industry conference. One of my favorite activities is something called "The Product Show." In a nutshell, teams compete against each other to ideate a make-believe product, brand it, pitch it and then write and sing a jingle about their spiffy product, to everyone's vast amusement.

At this conference, I was able to put people on teams who didn't know each other, or had heard of each other but had never actually met. The woman who hired me for the event participated in the exercise and, as it turned out, her team won the day. They were fantastic! They were cohesive and respectful of each other and they took joy in the exercise. As I was packing up for the evening, she took me aside to thank me for a stellar event. Then she did a "look left, look right" and leaned in. She told me that her team actually came up with another completely different product that they felt might really have a place in the market and they were going to form a company to see it to fruition!

100% true story.

 **Moving forward:**

Consider the teams you're on currently — at work, at home and/or in your community. Ask yourself these questions and be brutally honest with yourself:

1. Am I confident in the goals of my team(s)? If not, why and how do I better understand my team's goals?

2. Am I contributing my best skills and talents to this team? If not, why?

3. Do I listen or do I hear?

4. Do I make space for other people's views and ideas, even when they're (very) different from my own?

Chapter 11

Conflict is Scary and *Mostly* Necessary

Here we are — the chapter on CONFLICT. Maybe you rushed to read this chapter first. Perhaps you've put it off till last because you're big on conflict avoidance. No matter — you're here and it's time.

Before we jump in, I want to set the stage for this conversation: we're not talking about armed conflict or any facet of war or violence. It's not my expertise.

I would like to state for the record, that if we actually had more conversations, perhaps there would be less violent conflict.

But, again, not where this chapter lives.

This chapter is about the difficulties we have with each other personally. The goal for this section is to provide some insight on how to shift our perspective of common conflict, use it to our benefit, and perhaps even appreciate it. No weapons involved.

Well... no non-word weapons, you silver-tongued devil.

Conflict can be scary, especially when we're unprepared for it, and particularly with people we're not close to or don't know well. A sudden disagreement with our significant other over who added dirty dishes to the freshly-run-but-not-emptied-dishwasher isn't necessarily scary, though it may range very high on our aggravation meter.

Just the thought of disagreeing with someone can cause us to stress. Your heart beats faster, you feel warm, possibly sweaty. Your anxiety level rises. For most people, the path of least resistance is the road most traveled.

We avoid, we smooth, we lie and we allow.

But here's the pitfall — what you allow, is what will be.

I know a woman whose boss referred to her as "Lizzy." Her name was Elizabeth, and it was what she preferred and how she introduced herself to everyone. For months, it grated on her that her boss assumed a nickname that she hated, but she didn't say anything. At first, it was because he was her boss, and she was unsure how to correct him. She assumed that he'd hear everyone else call her Elizabeth and would catch on. He didn't. Time went on and she thought it would be weird to bring it up after months had passed. She ended up leaving her job and taking another position.

While the name issue wasn't the primary reason for her leaving, it did factor in her decision.

Keeping Elizabeth in mind, let's take a step back for a moment and understand in a really basic way, how conflict works.

One of the best, most bell-ringing lessons on conflict I've ever learned was from John Zinsser, Co-Founder of Pacifica Human Communications. He once said that conflict is not external. Conflict begins internally, and *we manifest it outside of ourselves.*

Conflict — all conflict — starts with our self-talk and the scripts we run in our heads. Or, as Brené Brown says, "the stories we tell ourselves."

In the case of Elizabeth, she felt her boss was being disrespectful to her by using a nickname. As time went on, that resentment grew and impacted her view of her work, management, and the company as a whole. That was the story she told herself — the script she had crafted. She doesn't *know* that her boss was purposefully being disrespectful because she never actually had a conversation with him about her dislike of the name Lizzy.

She manifested it in the one-sided way that we frequently have conversations in our head, and act on them as if those conversations were data and not supposition. To begin to get good at conflict, we have to ask ourselves this tough question: What is data and what am I assuming?

A couple of years ago, I was running a mixed gender workshop for about 15 customer service and sales professionals. At this particular session we were working on conversational competency and then moving on to some team-building exercises. In every workshop we run, people are at first, a little skeptical about what we're asking them to do. We purposely lead them to the land of discomfort and set up camp there for the day. The special sauce starts to kick in once the entire group, together, understands that no one person is (or will be) singled out, and that we're *all* going to do unexpected things.

While discussing conversation strategies, something wonderful happened. This group not only "got it" pretty quickly, but started digging in and asking some tough, in-depth questions about how to apply these skills to their work and personal relationships. It was an intense and thrilling conversation. Rarely has a group turned it around so quickly. This then led to a similarly intense conversation about conflicts and how to approach them.

What we discovered as a group was that until everyone involved understands that a conflict exists, we can't begin to deal with it. *You can't climb the mountain until you recognize there **is** a mountain.* We frequently overlook this component of our communication. We make assumptions. We make facts out of our personal scripts. Then we'll change our behavior or attitude towards the other person based on those scripts, while that person may have no idea that there's a problem.

In our workshop group, there were two people who had issues with each other, but neither really had a definitive reason as to why. During a break, and independent of each other, each of these people told me that they were viewing their difficulties in a new light, and were going to use the skills we had practiced to approach and communicate more effectively with each other. They each saw the mountain.

In the case of Elizabeth, had she done the thing that was momentarily uncomfortable — had a brief conversation with her boss about her name, rather than let the situation become untenable — the outcome might have been markedly different.

This brings us to our **1st Conflict Guideline:**

 Advocate for yourself as if no one else will.

Why is this so hard for people, especially women?

We're willing to continuously allow and to rationalize other people's behavior and actions to the detriment of our own lives and well-being.

And while the "why can't we all just get along?" mentality is *nice*, nothing can grow there.

You must advocate for yourself. You have to be your own champion, because *no one is coming to save you.*

I'm not suggesting you look for fights or jousts, or ultimate fighter competitions.

Advocating for yourself is <u>*acting*</u> on the belief that you have a place in the world that is no less important than anyone else's place in the world.

Yes, it's scary. Yes, it's necessary.

You're going to have to have conversations with people about how they treat you, speak to you, ignore you, refer to you, etc. Because, again, conflict begins internally, and most of the time, other people don't have a clue that we think something is "off" unless we tell them.

Keep in mind that we can't control other people. Read it again.

We cannot control other people.

You can *ask* them for change. You can't *make* them change.

You can change yourself.

Or, you can alter the situation — usually by exiting it. Those are the sum-total of your choices. Change yourself, breathe deep, and advocate for yourself by asking others for change, or exit.

So how do we actually have those cringe-inspiring, sweaty conversations?

First, talk about the thing that upset you, not that you're upset. You can't go to Bob or Karen with, "you've really pissed me off" and have that be the crux of the conversation.

Actually, "you've really pissed me off" is a BAD opening gambit. It immediately puts the other person on the defensive, and it makes someone else responsible for your feelings. They're not. They're yours. You're responsible, and entering a conversation in that way is like handing someone a platter of spoiled sushi and expecting them to be thrilled with it.

A more profitable way to broach a conflict conversation is to approach it from the perspective of seeking to understand.

For example, "Bob, it's possible I was unclear when we first met, but my name is Elizabeth and I really prefer that to Lizzy."

Certainly we can add a bit of humor to awkward or uncomfortable situations by acknowledging that they're awkward or uncomfortable.

For example, "Bob, I know this is a little weird after all this time, and it's possible I was unclear when we first met, but my name is Elizabeth and I really prefer that to Lizzy."

Chances are that Bob will immediately apologize, and will forevermore refer to you as Elizabeth.

There's a kind of template to these conversations:

I'd like to talk about {INSERT NAME OF CONFLICT HERE}.

It's my understanding {INSERT SHORT DESCRIPTION OF CONFLICT HERE}

I'd like to discuss a couple of solutions with you, namely {INSERT SOLUTION HERE}.

Hi Bob, I'd like to talk about the staffing in my department.

It's my understanding that the department appears to have a high rate of absenteeism.

I'd like to discuss some solutions the staff and I have come up with.

This isn't absolute or set in stone. The point is for you to find ways to have difficult or uncomfortable or even awkward conversations well. This is a jumping off place.

That bring us to our **2nd Conflict Guideline:**

 Find shared goals.

Remember the chapter on squad goals? All teams operate through shared goals.

If we cannot agree on a shared goal, regardless how large or small, our communication fails and we don't have a path to resolution.

So much conflict occurs because we don't have shared goals. Or we believe we don't have shared goals.

When we take the time to consider the conflict within ourselves, we may be able to find paths to resolution.

For example, I frequently use Saturdays to run errands and accomplish non-work related things. I have a list, an agenda, and a mission. When my daughter was 12, she and I did not have the same Saturday mission. It was ridiculously frustrating when I'd find that I've asked her for the 47th time to get something done and get her shoes on so we can leave the house, only to discover that she was side-tracked by a Lego puzzle and the thing isn't done, and the shoes are nowhere to be found. I realized that I had a choice. I could either let loose my frustration, holler and make us both feel bad or, I could breathe and consider that *my agenda is not her agenda*. We were not sharing goals, and that is huge.

Recognizing that I was frustrated and angry because my goals were being thwarted was just the beginning. Understanding that she felt exactly the same way was a blazing light of understanding. Once I created a situation where we were both going to get things that we wanted, including frozen yogurt, things moved quicker and easier.

If you've given the situation some thought, and understand where the difficulty actually originates, i.e. my agenda vs her agenda, you can then begin to create a path to shared goals.

Sometimes though, the goals get buried, feelings are hurt, we're pissed off and we can't see their point of view.

Shit happens. Again, people are hard. We're going to argue, maybe even fight (again, non-violently). We want understanding and we're willing to go to the mat to get it.

 There are PROFITABLE ways to handle conflict.

Profitable conflict is our **3rd Conflict Guideline.**

In this section, we're going to review the six "mandates" for profitable conflict.

No, we don't expect you to make money by fighting.

BUT, "profitable," meaning beneficial or helpful, could help you make more money, particularly if we're talking workplace conflict. Conflict negotiation skills are real, marketable attributes that companies want in their hires, because people who can successfully move through conflicts are people other people want to be around.

Conflict can be very good for us. It propels us forward, exposes us to new ideas and perspectives. Disagreement and discourse shows us where the work needs to happen. If everyone agreed all of the time, how bland, uninteresting and un-innovative we would be?

Some large organizations will use what's known as "The 10th Man Rule." In situations where consensus and everyone getting along can't provide a perspective to see all sides of a situation, one person is designated as the "loyal dissenter." It's their job to disagree for the benefit of the organization. The dissenter is the devil's advocate bucking the ideas of the group, in order to find the holes and pitfalls of those ideas.

The 10th man's role is to disagree profitably, and is necessary to understanding the issues from a variety of angles. In this case, conflict is literally the best thing for the organization.

Here are our **Six Mandates for Profitable Conflict**:

1. **Don't "name-call."** It's infantile and it doesn't move the conversation forward. It's hurtful and is nothing more than an expression of your frustration. Don't do it.

2. **Don't speak in absolutes.** It's easy when we're disagreeing with someone to blurt out "you always do that!" or "I never do that!" Speaking in absolutes is lazy and disingenuous. We live in grey areas, so make space for possibilities. Even if you're bone-sure that "always" or "never" are appropriate to the situation, speaking in an absolute doesn't allow for conciliation or empathy.

3. **Honor your boundaries.** We have boundaries for a reason. They are our "us-ness." Much of who you are is defined by what you do, what you're willing to do and what you allow.

   Boundaries are a hard-learned skill. We aren't born with an innate sense of what is right for us, or what is acceptable to us in the world. We learn over time and with countless hurts, experiences and exposures to the world, where our limits are and how we want the world to be.

We don't have to demand perfection from people. We can require that they do the best that they are capable. We can honor the imperfect humanity of others while respecting it in ourselves. Boundaries aren't necessarily lines in the sand. They're evidence of wisdom and growth and courage. They're proof of a life lived. The question you have to ask yourself when bumping against a boundary is "what comes next?"

4. **Pause & breathe.** Just stop. Stop speaking, stop yelling, stop (over) thinking for a moment, and pause. Then breathe. How many disagreements have you had that got ridiculously out of hand, quickly? It happens when we're hot and aggravated and frustrated. Escalation easily runs out of control and we're left saying or doing things we'll seriously regret after the fact. When you find yourself beginning to rise, stop for a moment and breathe. Offer that pause and breath to the person or people you're speaking with. Give everyone the opportunity to step back. It changes your energy and your tone.

My first post-college apartment was a tiny little hole in the Prospect Park area of Brooklyn that I shared with another actor. Though she and I were great friends, sometimes we argued. Strongly. To work through our disagreements, we devised something we called a "juice truce." When one of us knew that the conversation had devolved, no longer helpful or empathetic, we said the words "juice truce" and everything had to stop. Then we both went to the fridge and pulled out whatever juice or beverage we could find and drank a small glass. It was only after that pause and drink, that we could begin our conversation again, always with a different tone and a much calmer energy.

I've used a version of pause & breathe/juice truce ever since. It never fails to deescalate a situation.

5. **Peacemaking is not weakness.** It's easy to think of conflict in terms like "winner" and "loser," but that's rarely ever the case with humans. We live in a universe of grey and being empathetic to someone else's point of view is kind and valuable. Advocate for yourself, yes, *and*, work to see the other point of view so you can find the shared goals that may be buried in the words. That's strength and leadership.

6. **Be respectful of yourself.** This final guideline encapsulates all of the others. When you name-call or are purposefully cruel, you're being disrespectful of your own humanity because you're not honoring the humanity of others. Seek to be someone you're proud of even in your most difficult, clench-fisted, angry as a box of shaken bees, moments.

In our tip-toe through the fields of conflict, we've addressed perspectives and ideas that are relevant to both your work life and your "home" life. Let's shift for a moment and talk specifically about workplace conflict.

Where is our line in the sand?

We have to work with people.

No, you cannot act as singular overlord to your robot minions. At least, not yet. And while that day may come sooner rather than later, you still have to work with me. And them. And him, and all of the others you disagree with, don't like and just can't stand.

So how do we do it? How do we create and coalesce workplace teams and community with people we just don't get along with? We need to figure it out, and quickly, since flexibility/adaptability, creative thinking and working effectively in teams are the big-ticket skills of the 21st century workforce.

The most complex and simple answer to the question is that *we need to interact with people in order to learn how to interact with people.* Soft skills aren't easy to teach in a classroom with a slide show, a monotone presenter and a few dry sandwiches. Soft skills require people.

If you want to learn how to get along with difficult people, you have to practice. You have to try, repeatedly, to cross the divide. To begin, understand the difference between *don't get along with* and *can't work with.*

If you don't get along with someone, maybe there's a personality clash. You rub each other the wrong way. Maybe you don't like the way they speak to you, or they've snagged your clearly-marked lunch out of the break-room fridge one too many damn times. Whatever the difficulty, you can (and must) find a way to tolerate/accept/revise-your-view of the person in order to accomplish the shared goals. It won't be easy, because hey, XYZ person is uncool and you just don't like them.

Here's the thing: not everyone is for everyone. It's not wrong to not like someone.

Nobody can tra-la-la through life and expect to like everyone and to be liked by everyone. Humans aren't built like that. What we can do in this bigger picture, is allow ourselves to let go of liking someone so that we can go ahead and work with them. The two are not, necessarily, mutual.

The tougher problem is with someone you can't work with. Let's be clear, this means you are *unable* to create with this person. You've learned through time and experience that the two of you together are a combustible, toxic, unprofitable and uncommunicative combination, regardless of how you've built bridges and tried to span the chasm between you. The situation is untenable. If this is absolutely, positively the case, you have only a couple of options — the first being find another job. If you're put in a situation where you must work with someone (including a supervisor) who you absolutely, positively are unable to work with, get the hell out. The other alternative is an HR route — asking for a transfer, a different report, or a different departmental structure, etc., so that you can continue to work within the company but not with XYZ person. If that's not possible, see option A above.

Time is the main component in learning how to work with others. Great leadership and an awesome structure that makes you feel valuable and validated are parts of the mix. AND, it may be time to lean into your maturity and adulting skills, and get real about being open to points of view vastly different from your own. Understanding and empathy are vital soft skills that go along with profitable teamwork.

So, until the robot uprising (and maybe after...?), welcome to the world. Give peace a chance. And if that doesn't work for you, keep in mind you can learn as much, or more, from navigating a negative situation as you can from a positive.

 **For example:**

Agnes attended one of my public speaking bootcamps. She participated, learned and had a good time. A couple of weeks later, she reached out to initiate some one-to-one consulting. The bootcamp had opened her eyes to her communication "blind spots," and she was excited to move further out of her comfort zones.

In our work together, she described her tempestuous relationship with her sister. We worked together to help her craft more **profitable language** when interacting with her sister. She realized that their communication styles and personalities were very different and often clashed, causing hurt on both sides. She frequently asked her sister for change, with little success. After years of this kind of emotional warring, Agnes realized that the best way to **advocate for herself** was to exit the situation.

She made the painful decision to separate her life from her sister's life. The decision was one that brought pain, yes, *and* also a tremendous relief and the feeling of shucking a weight she didn't know she was carrying.

 Moving forward:

Ask yourself these tough-love questions:

1. Who in my life am I in conflict with right now?

2. Do I *know* why there is a problem, or is it a script I'm running in my mind?

3. Is it possible to have a conversation to resolve the issue with the person and ask for change? If so, begin to mentally plan that conversation and how you'd like it to go.

Consider the last disagreement or "fight" you had and dissect it.

1. Think about what specifically triggered the fight. Is that trigger reoccurring?

2. If so, what will you do differently the next time it happens?

3. Were you respectful of yourself during the disagreement or do you have regrets about things you may have said or done?

4. How will you plan to deal differently with your conflicts moving forward?

Chapter 12

This is Not a Book About Leadership, But Soft Skills Are Leadership Skills, So Maybe This is a Book About Leadership

I told you in the beginning that this book was not, necessarily, a deep dive into any one topic or skill.

This book is leverage. It's change. It's an opportunity.

I would be remiss and generally lacking if we didn't at least have a conversation about leadership skills, because…

Cue Card!

Not all leadership skills are soft skills, but ALL soft skills are leadership skills.

What makes a good "leader?"

For that matter, what makes a "leader?" Is it just a person who leads? I think no.

Being a "leader," and "leadership" and "good leadership" are those "basket" phrases that encapsulate a variety of skills, attributes and energy. Like "soft skills."

The word "follower" now has a slightly different connotation than the original definition intended. A famous person on social media, a so-called "influencer," may have millions of followers, but does that mean that they're a thought or industry leader? Or does it simply mean that that they are famous for being famous?

Being a leader means that other people look at you and look to you for guidance, information, cues on how to handle a situation and general getting-through-the-world information.

You don't "appoint" yourself as a leader. If you could, I hereby declare myself MOST BENEFICENT QUEEN OF ALL I SURVEY.

How do we define someone not only as a leader, but as a good leader? The definition has to be something more substantive than "…one who leads…" And so I've searched, and again, as we said in the beginning, there is a LOT of information out there on leadership. Between books, magazines, classes and fields of study, websites, ezines, posts and blogs, there is more information than any ten inquisitors could process in a lifetime. I slogged through much of it — what else would a beneficent queen do for the loyals?

What I've found is that there are studies and opinions, and studies about opinions, and much of that data is dependent on the times in which they were written. I also found a gazillion "Top 5" or "Top 10" listicles detailing traits or characteristics of a good leader, but nothing I felt was definitive… until now!

That's right, I've vetted and searched and strained and hammered my way to the list that ends all other lists:

The Top 5 Traits of Great (Seriously, Go Great or Go Home) Leaders

1. **Inspirational.** People have to follow you, and by follow, I mean they have to buy into you. This seems like a no-brainer but if you cannot share, convey and communicate your brilliance so that others want to join in, you're just a sad little engine without any boxcars or a caboose.

2. **Visionary.** You have a shareable vision. You have to know where you're going and basically how to get there. You can get lost, but don't be one of those folks who can't ask for directions. Vision includes shared goals and definitive strategies.

3. **Appreciative.** You must have the smarts and empathy to be grateful for people on the path with you. Alexander the Great always rewarded and acknowledged the guys in his troop who helped him claim and rename all those cities. Empathy is a huge part of appreciation and the culture that leaders create.

4. **Persistent.** You fail and get back up and keep going. You learn from the previous failures. Again, remember our two questions: What worked and is worth repeating? What needs improvement?

5. **Confident/Humble.** It's the old double-sided coin. You must be confident that what you're doing, where you're going and what you're building will actually work. You must be humble enough to realize you didn't do it, go there and build it alone.

There you have it, the absolutely definitive, slightly snarky list of what traits that makes a great leader.

 Leaders are role models.

They are people we want to emulate, to achieve like them and to follow in their footsteps.

Leadership also lives in the small skills. These are the less-talked about, less "sexy" skills that good leaders use and develop. Let's talk about four of them.

Saying "No" Well

We've all said "yes" to things we wish we hadn't. Even in the moment when we're forming the word "yes" with our mouth, our brain is saying, "nope, don't do it. You don't have time/energy/desire/interest to do this thing."

And yet, we said yes. And now we have to do the thing.

Or, we could be a shit and not do the thing we said we would do. We could string someone along saying that we're going to do the thing tomorrow, next week or next month. And then just not do it. AND, we expect someone to infer from the fact that we're *saying* one thing and doing *nothing* else that we're not actually going to do the thing. Sheesh, why won't they get a clue?! And then we ignore their calls and messages because we've talked ourselves into believing that somehow we're right, and they're just being a nuisance because *they expected us to do the thing we said we would do.*

This is how relationships are ruined.

Saying "no" well is a skill and an art. It's an honest way to give someone an answer they may not want, but deserve to have. It can preserve and expand your relationships.

There are profitable ways to decline.

First, be tactful. Let's say an organization that provides sweaters for small dogs asks you to sit on their board. If you're not a person who cares for dogs, clothing for dogs, knitting or crocheting, then this is not an opportunity for you. Your best approach is to let them know that you are honored to be asked. Thank them for that honor, and let them know that you are respectfully declining because it is not a cause you are passionate about. You don't have to tell them you think the idea is silly

Whatever you do, don't tell them that the *only* reason you're saying no is because of time. While that may be part of the truth, once they whip out the calendar and give you the lowdown on exactly how little time the commitment will take, you're stuck between a rock and a hard place. Once again, let them know that you're honored to be asked. Let them know that you've already allocated your time and resources elsewhere. You can say that you'd like to revisit the offer in six months or a year, if you're actually interested in doing the thing.

The final consideration to saying no well is ego. We don't want to hurt anyone's feelings, right? In every circumstance you must let the person know that you are honored to be asked. Ego is not a small consideration, both yours and theirs. If someone thought enough of your talent, expertise and reputation to make a request of you, you owe it to them to receive and decline that offer gratefully and graciously.

Saying no well can give you the opportunity to start conversations at a later date, to reconnect. It gives you the appeal of someone in demand. Resist the urge to say "yes" to something you don't enjoy, aren't enthusiastic about or just plain don't want to do. Nothing is so irksome and destructive as someone who doesn't keep a commitment.

Be Bold and/or Uncomfortable

Did anyone, anywhere achieve anything without first being bold in the idea or the ask, and then feeling uncomfortable in the doing?

We have big dreams. We want fame. Well fame costs, and right here's where you start paying, in sweat…

Big, bold dreams are what light the world. They are the ideas that send us forward in epic jumps. It's one thing to think boldly, but doing bold things very often means moving into the uncharted, risky and uncomfortable.

Doing and daring things you've never done before is difficult and uncomfortable. In the act of new-doing, we have to train our minds and bodies to be and act in unusual ways. It's unfamiliar. It's uncomfortable, and it's progress.

Growth, progress, or change is an uneasy proposition for most. Few people readily charge open-armed into a breach they've never visited before. We humans like our comforts. We enjoy our routines. There is safety in what we know, and yet, human beings are brilliant at adapting. We construct, we build and we circumvent. We solve the problem.

I know that when I've set out to do any great thing in my life, I've been *really* uncomfortable, sometimes even frightened. Failure, a lack of self esteem and the general unknown can create a heady brew of complacency. Don't drink it. Step away from the things and ideas that keep you in exactly the same place. Be bold.

Imagine some kind of discomfort meter pointed in your direction. Imagine it blipping wildly when you mentally view the thing that makes you uneasy. That wild mental blipping is how you know it's the thing that needs your attention the most.

Leaders must be bold. They are change makers, and they are the doers of new, difficult and uncomfortable things, because they're clearing the path. Whatever makes you uncomfortable, do it. Learn public speaking, be better at networking, grow your business, and be a better communicator. Challenge yourself to boldly revel in discomfort. Do it. Re-do it. Whatever it is. Whatever it takes. As Grace Hopper once said, "the most dangerous phrase in the language is 'we've always done it this way.'"

Embrace the Mistakes

A couple of years ago, I was running an elevator pitch workshop with a local college's graduate program. Unfortunately, there was a train stuck on the tracks directly in front of me, and regardless of my careful time management, I was 1/2 hour late to the event. And while the train debacle wasn't my *fault*, being late was my *responsibility*.

We are responsible for our choices. We are responsible for the effects and consequences of our choices and actions. We are accountable. As former President Harry S. Truman said, "the buck stops here."

We have to differentiate between fault and responsibility as well, and there is a difference. If you're in stop-and-go traffic and you decide to scroll through your emails and hit the car in front of you, then that's your fault, and your responsibility. If you're in the same traffic situation and the car behind you bumps you hard enough for you to bump the car in front of you, it's not necessarily your fault, but now you may bear some responsibility (caveat: not an insurance expert).

There is power in owning mistakes, gaffs, goofs and fuck-ups. You are where the buck stops. It speaks to integrity and trustworthiness. We must each be the leaders of our own lives.

Ask yourself, how much do you trust the person who is quick to accept credit when things go right, but never any blame when things go wrong?

Accountability can make the world better. Leadership, while it may be bold, is imperfect. By acknowledging what/when we've done wrong, we give ourselves the ability to be thoughtful and to do better next time, and we show that to others. The world needs more of that leadership.

Setting All the Goals

We're calling "goal setting" a small skill because it falls under the idea that leaders are visionaries, and a vision must have a road map. Otherwise it's just a fluffy dream.

Like "leadership," there is a wealth of information available on "goal setting." Again, we're taking a slightly smaller view.

I participated in an event once where the speaker introduced us to the "BHAG" or "Big Hairy Audacious Goal." I really love how descriptive that term is and the visual it conjures in my brain.

But, what if we change perspectives a bit. Maybe, just maybe, the key to achieving goals isn't *just* to have BHAGs, but to better understand the processes we use to get big and hairy.

As a young actor, my professors taught me how to break down a script into scenes and beats. They taught me to develop a process to move through the words on the page and to create a living, breathing and believable human being. Because it is a process, it's repeatable for every script, regardless of genre, venue, writer or costars. I have taken to calling this "Big Goal, Little Goal" (BGLG).

I put off writing this book for years because the thought of A BOOK was too daunting. What allowed me to achieve this giant, hairy thing in front of you was a bit of guidance and small moves — organizing my materials, creating working chapter titles, putting that information into an outline, etc.

BGLG is applicable to life. It is the process of accomplishing little tiny, micro goals that move you forward to accomplishing the next level of goals. Deodorant is an excellent example of Big Goal, Little Goal.

Let's say you set a goal to get a promotion (and accompanying raise) at work by the end of the year. In order to make that happen, you understand that you have to show up at work, participate, engage and be a generally stellar and contributing human. Showing up requires that you transport yourself from your home to your job. Before you complete that transport, you have to awaken on time, shower, dress and eat a little something. Hopefully, for all our sakes, deodorant is an integral part of the dressing process. It's a key ingredient in putting together your personal presentation, which can affect your confidence, which can directly affect how you are perceived, which directly affects the value you are thought to bring, which can have a direct and substantial affect on the promotion and raise goal.

Deodorant. It can change the world.

This is the beauty of BGLG. When you step back from the gargantuan, Herculean task of ACHIEVEMENT and create the processes by which you get from "A" to "A.5" instead of to "Z," your intentions and ambitions become more manageable and more easily attained. Putting on deodorant is a necessary and valuable step in world domination.

Go ahead. Dream of the BHAG. Think of the world you want to exist. Then build the processes one tiny, little structural baby goal at a time. And if you forget the deodorant, the stink is all on you.

BONUS "Small" Skill: Filling the Well

Can we talk about self-love for a moment?

What I mean is the action we take to consciously care for and prepare ourselves to move forward in the world. It's how we "fill the well."

I've been labeled an introvert, and while I don't think that any one label defines a person, I agree that conceptually, I'm introvert. I derive my energy from being alone. I enjoy socializing and game nights and group activities and the feeling of connectedness I get from those activities. Then, I want to be by myself and to be quiet. It is my way to recharge and to revitalize. It's how I refill my well.

There are times, though, when I have to draw deeper. These are times when I've found myself feeling angry and stressed all the time, even about seemingly unimportant things. It's during those times that I realize it's been a long while since I'd given myself a time out.

A couple of years ago, I was facing one of those times. Nothing in my life was dramatically different. There were no exceptional events happening, but I wasn't functioning at my highest level. Not even close. The five thousand balls I have juggled for years threatened to rain down on my head. So, I made a conscious decision to fill my own well. I booked a local oceanfront hotel for two solitary nights in the middle of the week. I brought food to stock the mini-fridge, enough reading material to last weeks and my flip flops.

The timing was terrible, but it was always going to be terrible because life wasn't going to stop without me. My husband, my daughter and my business all needed my attention and still, I took the exit anyway. And it was glorious. I had time to walk along the water. I made the opportunity to read and to sit and watch the whole sunset as it happened. I reached a silent truce with a cranky dock cat whose territory I kept unintentionally invading. I chatted with strangers around a gorgeous fire and left when I felt like leaving. I was inspired. I breathed, I slept and watched bad TV, and I filled my well.

As I drove home, I had a clearer picture of how I was going to deal with several issues I had been contemplating for weeks. I had new ideas. I felt peaceful and happy to return to my life. I felt like I could juggle again.

I empowered myself by knowing who I am.

If all of this sounds privileged, it is. If it sounds selfish, perhaps it is, but consider this: on an airplane, you're told to put the oxygen mask on yourself first and then put the mask on someone else. In order to be my best self, and continue to lead my family and business, I had to help myself. I needed to be alone, quiet and contemplative. It's what I require, and I know it's not what everyone requires. Some people recharge by being with crowds of people, by constantly interacting with others and receiving that energy. Those people thrive on sound and movement. I know this because I married that person, but I am not that person.

If you can understand who you are, how you derive your energy and what you need to fill your own well, then you can empower others do the same. Leaders must lead by example. Understanding how you function and become your best self is an excellent way to set a great example.

UPDATE: I'm writing this particular segment from knee-deep in the COVID-19 pandemic. We've been quarantining and limiting our human contact for many months. My husband's job hasn't much changed, except for more protective gear, but my daughter and I have been home together the entire time.

Let me repeat that. The. Entire. Time.

We chose to have her learn virtually, so she's been completing her 10th, and now 11th grades, at our kitchen counter. Clearly not an ideal situation, but it is the situation we're in.

So how does a person who's idea of refueling self-care is being alone, handle never actually being alone?

I wake up earlier than everyone else. I go for dark early morning walks alone. I've begun meditating. You might laugh, but whoo boy, I think it's saved me more than once in dealing with daughter and husband conflicts.

I've created time and a boundaried space (my closed office door) where I don't have to talk to anyone, I don't have to *do* for anyone and, if I'm totally honest, the bra is flung on the one of the office guest chairs and I scroll through Instagram like a boss. Ahhh, that's good leadership.

I've encouraged my daughter to find creative ways to deal with her well-being too. She spends time firmly ensconced in her room singing, dancing, creating new fashion and general teenager-ing. She paints and draws everyday. And while she, too, is missing the social component of being human in the world, she does have "safe" friends she can be with.

It is imperfect, and it's good. We're each refilling and refueling as we can, where we can, with what we can.

What we need now is a break from the world.

What we think of as leadership is acted out and proven with a variety of small and large skills. It is attitude and belief. It is showing up, again and again, even when the shit is hitting the fan. It is constantly considering the path and tweaking it as you go.

Good leadership is imperfect. History is riddled with people we call "great" leaders who made catastrophically bad decisions. It's the recovery that evidences character. We admire the people who fall down and get up again, for good reason. They learn, they listen and they do.

So, here's the best leadership advice you might ever read: **Do the next right thing, and wear deodorant while doing it.**

 **For example:**

Scene #1: R. H. Macy — Founder of Macy's department store. Mr. Macy, who lived in Massachusetts, opened four different dry-goods stores, all of which failed. In 1858 he moved his family to New York City and opened a new store on the corner of Sixth Avenue & 14th Street. The location turned out to be an excellent choice. He successfully experimented with offerings that other stores didn't have, like a Santa Claus, a larger variety of departments and themed window displays. Macy's eventually became the "largest store on Earth." Side note: the red star in the Macy's logo is based on a tattoo Mr. Macy got on his hand while working on a whaling ship.

Scene #2: James Dyson — Inventor of the Dyson Cyclonic Bagless Vacuum. Faced with the problem of his vacuum cleaner's diminishing performance, he realized that if he could find a way to eliminate the bag, he'd have a much better product. It took more than five years, almost all of his savings and 5,126 prototypes to create a vacuum that didn't lose suction. Unfortunately, he still couldn't get anyone to manufacture his product, so he created his own manufacturing and research company. Today, his net worth is valued at somewhere around $4.8 billion dollars.

Scene #3: Grandma Muddle — For most of her life, my Gram was the definition of a housewife. She cooked, cleaned, ironed, scrubbed, shopped and generally served my grandfather. She didn't work outside of the home, and my grandfather handled all the money, giving her a weekly "allowance." When he got sick and died, my grandmother had to learn new skills from the ground up. She had to open bank accounts, learn to write a check and pay bills to keep herself afloat. She expanded her world. She became more active in her church, and in her eighties was driving meals to home-bound "old" people. She baked special Halloween treats for the neighborhood kids, and survived cancer three times. She smiled and was joyful, and when she held your face in her hands, you knew you were loved.

She reveled in her life, her faith and the people she could help. When she died at 93, a huge portion of our hometown came out to the service. She was kind to everyone and she led by a shining example. Her generous heart, loving spirit and spine of steel have had a profound effect on my life and the legacy I'd like to achieve.

 Moving forward:

1. Who do you admire and or consider a good/great leader? Why?

2. What is it about their character, performance or achievements do you take inspiration?

3. What leadership traits and skills do you possess? Can you identify leadership skills that you're lacking? What do you need to work on?

4. Decide on two specific leadership skills you're going to work on for the next month. Make a plan (goal-setting anyone?) on how you're going to achieve growth in those areas.

For example: You know you need to work on accountability. Decide on a specific project that you're going to complete. Let your friends and/or co-workers know what you're doing. Give yourself a deadline for completion. Create a plan to complete your project within the timeframe and to the best of your ability. Then, at the deadline, when your project is completed with bold brilliance, slap yourself on the back and pop the champagne because you achieved progress!

Mmmm, that's stellar leadership.

Chapter 13

BUT WAIT, THERE'S MORE!

As we discussed in the beginning, there is an almost incalculable list of soft skills we could name and work on when dealing with our personal and professional growth. In these pages, I've given you what I think are some of the big hitters and a few of the smaller fries.

Mixed metaphors anyone?

You've now received enough information to grow your skills to mountainous heights, and yet, I have more for you.

What can I say, I'm a giver.

What follows is a buffet of ideas and perspectives you can use to grow your skills. These are little vignettes designed to offer you a mental springboard to consider, expand and implement into your soft skills library. This is a smörgåsbord of sorts. A veritable feast for your heart and your head.

Enjoy!

Keeping Your Word

Is keeping your word a soft skill?

What do you call it? What's the word for keeping your word? As an avowed word geek, I can give you 15 synonyms for "promise," but none of them seems exactly right. Is a promise still a promise if you don't say the words, "I promise," or is it just "keeping your word?"

We see a lot of "oath-breaking" these days. I know, it sounds very *Game of Thrones*, but there it is. Countries who were thought to lead the world pull out of established agreements, presidents present "alternative facts," social contracts are broken by people calling the police on other people because of a barbecue, couples get divorced and people lie right to your face.

When did doing what you said you were going to do become so damn difficult? Is this a bygone concept, something that no longer has a place in this global, digital world? If we cannot stand in our word, is it the end of civilization as we know it?

I recently had a conversation with my teenage daughter on this very subject. She told me that she would do something in a period of time and the thing did not get done. When I asked her about it and said that she had given me her word, she responded with, "no, I said I'd do it but I didn't promise." She couldn't tell me the difference between the two except the actual pronouncement of the words, "I promise." Evidently there are levels of truthfulness of which I was unaware of.

There is honor in doing what you say you will do, and personal accountability. It goes along with trustworthiness and strength of character. If you can't stand in your words truthfully, then you create distrust and chaos around you. Perhaps we don't *mean* to not keep our word, it's just easier and more comfortable, not to. If keeping your word is a soft skill, it's a hard one.

Here's how this works… You say you will, and you *do*, in a timely manner. Don't make someone chase or hound you. If it ends up you cannot do the thing, say so, again, in a timely manner. Be honest. Don't avoid. Don't ghost. Don't be that guy. Abide by the contracts, social and otherwise, that make a civilization civil. If you have reason to protest them, do so with integrity. These are the things we can learn and practice and teach.

As for me, maybe I didn't say, "I promise," but I did say I would and between them is no difference at all.

Never Underestimate the Power of a Good Handshake

In-person meetings with a prospective client, employer or investor is premium time (post COVID-19). Why would you want to make a first impression that includes a bad hand handshake? Hopefully, you wouldn't knowingly fail at shaking hands, so let's review.

Handshakes are literally a way to bring someone close to us, so we can begin to decide if we want to continue interacting. You probably wouldn't halt a meeting after someone offers you a limp shake, but you absolutely file it away mentally in the "CON" column.

It's thought that handshakes originated to show the other person that you didn't have a weapon and that you had no ill intent. So consider this — when shaking hands with someone, you bring them close enough to look them in the eyes and to smell them. Sounds odd, but remember that scent is the sense most closely tied to memory, so the nose knows. It's a way to be intimate, without being *intimate.*

Handshakes should be firm without being bone-crunching. It's not (usually) an athletic contest. Offer your full hand, not just the tips of the fingers. No one, and I mean <u>no one,</u> enjoys a limp and/or moist handshake. And since you're not getting water from a well, don't pump. One or two up/down movements and you're golden. According to History.com, there is a Victorian-era guide that cautions, "a gentleman who rudely presses the hand offered him in salutation, or too violently shakes it, ought never to have an opportunity to repeat his offense."[13] This goes for women as well.

When I was growing up, my dad would comment after the fact if someone gave him a bad handshake. It immediately downgraded his opinion of the person. In the digital age, when personal meetings take on extra levels of importance and time is money, make sure that you're always offering your best hand forward.

Civility Costs You Nothing

Kindness, respect and civility. These qualities are the cornerstone of soft skills and the basis for profitable human connection. We admonish our children to "be good." We teach them manners as a basic interaction tool, and we tell them to treat others as they wish to be treated. It's time we adults took our own advice to heart.

Civility costs nothing. There is no toll to be paid for civility, and yet we adults frequently log situations where kindness and civility are excused. Road rage is a perfect example. Or forwarding internet memes designed to demean people — they're okay, 'cause it's funny and it's just a joke.

How about when someone is uncivil to us?

Did you forget to thank me for holding the door? I now have carte blanche to call you an asshole, out loud. Apply that turn signal a little

13 Andrews, Evan. "The History of the Handshake". history.com. 2016, Updated 2020. https://www.history.com/news/what-is-the-origin-of-the-handshake

too late (or not at all?), eh? I'm just gonna speed up and flip you off, so you know who's boss, etcetera, etcetera.

Dismiss these skills as "soft" or even as unnecessary to our success, at your own peril. In the simplest terms, when we feel disrespected or are treated unkindly, it makes us feel bad and we don't perform at our best, particularly at work. Georgetown Professor Christine Porath, who has amassed a staggering amount of data and research on the effects of incivility in the workplace, writes,

> *Of the nearly 800 managers and employees across 17 industries Christine Pearson of the Thunderbird School of Global Management and I polled, those who didn't feel respected performed worse. Forty-seven percent of those who were treated poorly intentionally decreased the time spent at work, and 38% said they deliberately decreased the quality of their work. Sixty-six percent reported their performance declined and 78% said their commitment to the organization had declined.[14]*

Imagine the impact respect, kindness and civility have on the bottom line of a company, organization or even a personal relationship. There is a domino effect: by making people feel valued and listened to, we in turn feel valued and a tone is set. Incivility breeds more of the same. Bosses who abuse their authority or belittle others will create that on-going, unprofitable drama. Being good at something doesn't give you a pass to be a lousy human.

Kindness and civility may cost nothing, but it does take an effort. We have to be more aware of ourselves and how we deal and cooperate with people. We literally have to treat others as we want to be treated and not pay lip service to that idea. In a survey conducted by the Born

---

14 Porath, Christine. 2017. "The Silent Killer of Workplace Happiness, Productivity and Health is a Lack of Basic Civility." Quartz. https://qz.com/1079344/the-silent-killer-of-workplace-happiness-productivity-and-health-is-a-lack-of-basic-civility/?utm_source=dlvr.it&utm_medium=facebook

This Way Foundation[15] (Lady Gaga's undertaking), 3,000 teens, young adults and parents found that mental wellness is dramatically impacted by being around or close to, kind people. There is a logic to it. The Golden Rule is gold for a reason.

 Treating people with kindness and civility creates a positive ripple effect.

Kindness, respect and civility are not always easy. Sometimes it's hard damn work to maintain civility in the face of unkindness. Lashing out or acting back may feel really, *really* good, for a moment… but, character is not made up of what someone else does, but how we react to it.

I Appreciate You

While we're on the subject, everybody wants to be loved.

People, companies, and the color purple all want to know that you appreciate what they offer.

In the big picture, it actually costs us nothing to be appreciative. It doesn't diminish us or make us look weak. It doesn't lesson our stature. In fact, it's one of those easy skills that draw people to us. Who doesn't want to work for or with a company that outwardly loves its talent and rewards their customers for being customers?

Who doesn't want to spend time with a friend or family member who likes you and values you for who you are?

15 Gibbs, Adrienne. July 27, 2017. "Want to Improve the Workplace? New Research by Lady Gaga's Foundation Quantifies Kindness." Forbes. https://www.forbes.com/sites/adriennegibbs/2017/07/27/want-to-improve-the-workplace-new-survey-by-lady-gagas-foundation-quantifies-effects-of-kindness/?sh=644c6d2e6792

I certainly want to spend time with people who appreciate and honor the talents I bring to the table.

Find ways to sincerely acknowledge the efforts of others, whether it's great or small. Be encouraging, not manipulative. When you allow yourself to be authentically grateful, you might find that you, your team and/or your company, actually have much about which to be grateful.

Showing Up is Great, But Being Engaged Makes You Relevant

We put a premium on attendance. We'll provide certificates and trophies to kids who don't miss a day of school or who attend every soccer practice. At work, we'll hoard personal time or extoll the nose-to-the-grindstone-ness of the employee who hasn't taken a vacation in years. And while attendance is great, you know, it's fine, it doesn't clock actual participation.

Showing up may be half the battle, but what's the point? In the scheme of a life, why just "show up?" Why attend if all you're doing is a lap, a smile and an exit?

Engaging is scary. It takes work, personal effort and maybe some discomfort, but it is the color of existence. Engaging is the entire point of being.

The framework doesn't matter — work, relationships, beliefs. I know people who have worked at a place for a lengthy amount of time. They do their work, they'll complain about others and they go home. They don't actually do anything to fix the situation or offer solutions. They operate within a small box and never outside it. They show up and they're mostly disconnected. Some people live the same way in their relationships. They'll go years without communicating with children or spouses. It's easier. It's a non-choice. These same people will lament world events, politicians and leaders but will do nothing more than shake their fists at the screen.

Get up, dress up and show up used to be all that was asked of you, but no longer.

The world requires you to connect, engage and participate. We are each a universe unto ourselves with singular experiences, views and perspectives. We need your you-ness. It is time to be present.

To participate is to sometimes fail, and that is a grand, good and colorful thing. It's important and should be done frequently. Don't overthink it. Just speak up. Speak out. Offer a solution. Make the call. Dance. Greet the stranger. Take a stand. Connect.

Stop being irrelevant.

Manage My Damn Customer Service Expectations

We're all customers.

If you work, you're also in customer service. It doesn't matter if you never see or speak to an actual client or customer, you're in customer service. You, as an employee of a business, any business (especially if it's your business), represent that business and its brand in the world. You are a customer service person.

We've all had moments when we absolutely had to ask for the manager, or at least a person in charge. I recently had a ridiculous text exchange with a customer service person about the $0.53 sales tax difference in an item I was returning and re-purchasing in a different size. After several labored exchanges where the person repeatedly told me they had no idea why there was a difference, but still offered a number of outlandish reasons (i.e. a $0.03 difference in shipping costs triggered a $0.53 sales tax difference), they finally offered me free shipping — a savings of over $8. I happily agreed.

If you've ever been on the serving side of a customer service conversation, and have faced the brain fever mania that can affect some people, you have an understanding of how wrong these conversations can go.

Some people are terrible, will always be terrible, and will look for opportunities to be terrible to others. Leaving those people aside, there are ways to give (better) customer service, regardless of your actual position.

First, ask questions and then actually listen to the answers. Use the information they've provided to further the conversation. The goal is satisfaction. Actually, the goal is a repeat customer.

Give real information. Don't guess, or hypothesize. Give people <u>data</u> that resolves the issue.

Be pleasant. You would think this should go without saying, but no, no it doesn't. We all have terrible days when it feels like everything we touch turns to mush. A person speaking kindly to us is a boon. I was waiting in line at the bank once and overheard a harried woman tell the teller that she was "…a bright spot in a terrible day." Be that.

Finally, honor their time. If you say you're going to deliver on a certain date, at a certain time, do that. Don't lose my reservation. Don't tell me fairy tales. Don't lie to me.

A word about the flip side: Just because you have a grievance/issue/problem/hang nail, it does not give you carte blanche to be a terrible, awful person. Looking at you, Karen, looking at you.

The Big Ask: Help Me

I don't need help, I can do it by myself.

I used to think that doing it all by myself was a sign of strength, of toughness and of will. I now know, in my wizened years, that I was full of shit.

Understanding that you may not have all the answers is growth. Problem-solving is a skill, and realizing that other people's experiences and abilities are tools that we can utilize, is life-altering.

As children, we're praised and celebrated for learning to do things on our own. We've accomplished something when we can dress and feed ourselves, by ourselves. These "existence" skills are integral to our placement as contributing members of society. As we grow up, we supplement our existence skills by learning a wide variety of pertinent and valuable societal skills. We've solved many of our needs-based problems by becoming a consuming economy. We buy groceries because we don't have the time, inclination or ability to grow our own food. We require that "help" in order to survive, and in return, we offer monetary compensation.

But what happens when we just can't get it done? When what's being asked of us or required from us, is simply too much, too hard, too unknown for us to fathom alone?

Do we curl into a ball and wish for a solution?

Do we stand and live in our frustration, ignorance and inability, shaking our fists at the sky until some random person or entity comes to save us?

No, and do you know why?

No one is coming to save you.

You have to save yourself, and that may mean you'll have to ask for help. It sounds contradictory, but it's not. Looking for assistance is a profound act of self-care and progress. It can be as easy as joining a Facebook group dedicated to women professionals and typing a post looking for a particular piece of advice. It can be as effortless as stopping your co-worker on their way to the restroom and asking them which typeface is punchier. It can also be as thick and dark as tottering on the edge of depression and actually keeping an appointment with a counselor.

My father, who was absolutely **not** a religious man, would often shrug when we expressed frustration at a problem and tell us that "God helps those who help themselves, how will you help yourself?" He didn't want to rescue us, but to teach us that asking for help is appropriate and thoughtful. Whining about the problem wasn't.

We often are much kinder to others then we are to ourselves. Stop that. Look around. The Universe *wants* to help you.

 Asking for aid is not weak, it's self-care.

Needing help doesn't mean you're incapable or unqualified. It simply means that you're a human looking to fill in some gaps. Seeking help, regardless of how teeny tiny or gargantuan the problem might be, is a powerful act of forward motion. Save yourself, make the ask.

The Innovation Confabulation

"The most damaging phrase in the English language is 'We've always done it this way.'"

This quote by Rear Admiral Grace Murray Hopper nutshells how damaging, and perhaps dangerous, stagnant thinking can be. We gain, we profit and we move by innovating, by asking ourselves hard questions.

Imagine the scene where our human forepeople first had the idea of putting the wheel and a horse together. Maybe it was an accident or maybe it was curiosity... "Say, Bob, I know this sounds crazy, but what if, and walk with me here a moment, we tethered old Blackie there to my wheelbarrow and let him pull the stones, hmmm?"

What? It could have happened like that.

Curiosity is the point.

I was hit with the "...that's how I've always done it..." phrase when explaining to my daughter why she should try doing something in a different (read: my) way. It opened an interesting dialogue about innovation and creative problem solving — a conversation I'm always happy to have.

I've been pondering this sort of war between "If it ain't broke, don't fix it," and "There has to be a better way!" for years. Are people firmly fixed in one camp or the other? I know some people are happily entrenched in their attitudes, ideas and daily accomplishments and are simply not open to anything new or slightly different, because different is uncomfortable. Even if it's helpful and solves a problem, it's just easier to keep doing what they've always done.

Why is that? Is it fear? Is it laziness?

Then there's the flip side: someone who is constantly tinkering and fixing so that there is no consistency at all. This lack of consistency and constancy is viewed as unreliable, or not committed to the task or objective. So where do we find the middle ground?

We humans are born innovators. We exit the womb ready to try, learn, fail and repeat. We are inherently creative. We had to be to survive. But it's the little failures over time that break us — the tiny stress fractures of life that close us off and make us unwilling to create or overcome. The effect is that our world becomes fractionally smaller, constantly. We create a space for ourselves where we don't have to create or be challenged. For many of us, all is rote, and it's safe.

Except that it's not and "safety" is a lie.

We live in an ever-shifting set of circumstances. Your routine may not seem to change, but the world around it fluxes every minute of every day, and that impacts you. Simply put, if there is a change in the shell, it affects the yoke.

We're living an example of this with the COVID-19 pandemic.

What if you're not creative — that not being innovative isn't a function of laziness, but an actual lack of creativity? The good news is that it doesn't matter if you're not a painter or sculptor or a tech guru. You can learn innovation. Author and Stanford Professor Tina Seelig posits an "innovation engine," whereby there is a structure to learning creativity. It starts with asking questions and challenging ourselves to keep asking questions, and challenging the questions themselves.

Questions are the middle ground between "…always done it this way…" and "…let's change it again…" Questions are where we find our creativity, our innovation and connections to each other.

Remember in a previous chapter we talked about "What if?" Innovation and creativity are born around "What if?"

Because you've "…always done it this way…" doesn't answer a question, nor does it ask one. Be curious. Find your curiosity, because curiosity leads to knowledge, and knowledge leads to more questions.

It's one of the reasons you're reading this book.

 Moving forward:

Pick one small skill. Choose any one skill of these small, buffet-table skills we've listed here, and work on that one.

Examine where your skill range is now, and where you'd like it to be in the future. Set a goal for change. How will you measure that growth? What does that growth look like to you?

For example: Let's say you choose to be more civil. First, when do you think, or have been told, that you're at your most uncivil? Begin your work at those moments. Mostly likely, they occur when you're angry, upset or frustrated. Remind yourself that you can do better — that raising your voice or name-calling doesn't actually achieve anything. Create a mantra that you can repeat to yourself in times of stress and incivility. Think: "I'm a Zen mother-fucker. I'm a Zen mother-fucker." Breathe. Pause. Do better.

Goal achieved.

Chapter 14

In Conclusion: Singular Spectacular-ness Lies Within

In the beginning, I proposed that we learn together and that perhaps, this book might not be for you, but you're here.

You've made it through, and hopefully you found there was a little something for you contained in these pages — a little nugget of golden "aha!" or a moment of clear blue self-awareness, and, I hope, a good sideways laugh.

If, in the process of reading this book, you've given thought to the real people talked about in its pages, looked at their journeys and saw yourself, kudos to you!

If you've found real and actionable ways to grow your skills and/or the skills of the people you lead, kudos to me.

You are exactly who I wrote this book for. Thank you for joining me on the journey.

And touching the creamy centers.

Here is what I know...

I spent the first many years of my young (and then not-so-young) adult life honing my creative and theatrical crafts. I acted in, directed and produced stage shows, a tiny movie and a radio show. I built costumes and sets. I designed choreography. I ALSO worked at some of the most prestigious legal and financial firms in the country. I helped catch counterfeiters for one of the most prestigious fashion houses in New York. I've taught scuba diving. I've gotten married and birthed a baby. Now I run a company. I have had an unparalleled experiential life education.

As an actor, I grew my confidence, my resiliency, my ability to speak well and my observational skills. As a woman in business, I've used all of those theatrical skills working with a wide variety of people, learning to negotiate, communicate and thrive in high-stress situations. I've refined an ability to observe and profitably process the conversations — verbal and non-verbal, that we're constantly having with other humans.

Observation is my superpower.

I would have liked the ability to fly, but we are who we are...

I grew up believing nothing was expected of me because I had no value. I learned to rewrite the scripts of my childhood. It's an ongoing process.

Learning and working in the theatre gave me life. My theatre training afforded me the opportunity to step outside of my tiny box, to shift my perspective and to see the world and my place in it, on a much larger scale.

And then I chucked it all to go teach scuba diving in Mexico.

But that's a whole other story.

I built my company around the idea that through theatre strategies — engaged and creative play, observation and application — everyone could grow their skills to be the *best version* of themselves. It has been my joy to work with an amazing array of people and a variety of companies who chose to get a little uncomfortable. These are people and organizations that opt-in to looking at the world a bit differently, to play and fail, and play some more. There is little in life that is more exciting to me than a person who shifts because of work we've done together.

That's what I want for you. It's what I want you to want for you.

I want you to be the best damn version of yourself that you can be. I want you to seek out the uncomfortable places. It's your job to take hard, steely-eyed looks at where you've been so you can see more brightly, where you can go.

Small changes. Small awarenesses. New, better conversations. This is how the world changes, and how stronger and more inclusive systems are built.

No matter where you are in your life, regardless of what terribleness, joy and beauty lay behind or is still to come, IF you've read these pages and IF you're willing to be more thoughtful about how you move through the world, IF you're ready to take charge of your words — to yourself AND out loud, and IF you actually practice doing things just a little bit differently, then, by all of the rights and powers bestowed on me as the author, I pronounce you more SPECTACULAR.

Not that you weren't already...

Understanding and utilizing great soft skills can only benefit you. There is zero down-side to being a more conscious and conscientious communicator. You get to have better, more profitable conversations. Juicy conversations about money and the skills you possess and how valuable they are to a business, or *your* business. Tough conversations about your place in the world and how you decide the world will interact with you.

You can stress less by advocating for yourself and your boundaries through uncomfortable, yet authentic conversations. By carefully observing the world in front of us, and observing how we think and react to that world, we can grow our empathy for ourselves and others.

And yoga. I understand that yoga is good for you.

Changing the world, changing your life isn't necessarily the act of moving giant boulders. It's picking up small pebbles, one at a time, shaping and carrying them to a new place. That's growth and *shift*.

Small awarenesses are the foundation of epic transformation.

I want to leave you with one of my favorite "listicles." It sums up and repeats many of the key points of this book because this is a creative studio and we always ask "what works and is worth repeating?"

And because all the world's a stage and communication is everything.

10 Things Actors Know That You Don't...Or Didn't Until Now

Working for years in the theatre, you pick up a few things. Not only props and costumes but information and observations that are easily translatable to other venues. It's amazing how much of what I learned as an actor, director and producer is compellingly applicable to business and work life. Here are 10 communication growth hacks actors know that you don't:

1. When speaking or presenting, rehearse, rehearse, and rehearse. Then, rehearse some more. When speaking to a group of two or one thousand, know your material!

2. Once you know your material as well as you know your own name, (see #1 above), forget trying to think about the actual words. We call this "organic," meaning that the words come from the energy of the moment. Once the words are so ingrained, you don't have to stress about finding them and speaking becomes more natural — like a conversation as opposed to a recital. This allows you to be a better, more natural and engaged speaker.

3. **Every** meeting is an audition.

4. Every audition is a chance for success or failure, but sometimes, and this is important to remember, it may have absolutely nothing to do with you. You may be brilliant. You may be exactly what they need, and yet, they didn't pick you. You may never know the actual reason why they didn't pick you. It's out of your control, so control what you can, be your most awesome self, and let the rest go.

5. When you're not speaking, you are still communicating. My dog doesn't actually "speak" to me (well, nothing I can repeat here…), but she sure can communicate what she wants ("a biscuit please," "love me, love me, love me") and needs ("outside, NOW!"). Actors know that humans speak more, and loudest, when not actually talking.

6. When speaking publicly, particularly for the first time in a venue, please, please get there early to suss out the space. Few things are more important than getting the lay of the land — where are you in relation to the audience? Where is the sound coming from? Will they have a podium or a table to put your notes on? How far from the space is the restroom? Will there be snacks? All very important items of note.

7. Stop talking and listen. I've said this 52 million times and I'll continue to say it — time spent listening is time very well spent. Don't act like you're listening when you're actually mentally compiling your next witty interjection. Sit back, look at the person and hear the words; hear the way they're saying the words. Listen to their energy when they're speaking.

8. Use "Yes, and…" A negative interjection often derails a conversation or sends it in a completely different direction. By using this ground-floor basic of improv artistry, you can encourage greater dialogue, even if you don't 100% agree with what's being said.

9. Listen to what they're not saying. Humans communicate huge amounts of information without saying a word. It's these non-verbals that very often clue us into the person we're speaking with. Believe what they do, not *necessarily* what they say.

10. Lift your head and speak. Seems like a no-brainer. It's not. Stop looking at the ground and mumbling. Actors know that regardless of amplification system, the voice is an instrument. Use it well by breathing, lifting your chin, using proper diction and making eye contact.

Epilogue: Inspiration, Aspiration and Listicles

As with humans, soft skills don't always fit into a nifty little box. Sometimes you need an epilogue. One that's full of easy and dare we say, fun, ways to consider your skills.

What follows are some valuable bits and pieces.

Infrastructure: 11 Soft Skills Truisms

1. People will judge you and you will judge others. Character is built by both.

2. Listening will get you much, much further than talking.

3. Being too empathetic is not a thing.

4. Hone your public speaking skills — they'll serve you your entire life.

5. Conflict begins internally.

6. Negotiation is fluid, not fixed.

7. Don't be afraid to ask for what you want.

8. Learn to speak well about yourself as well as others.

9. Understand your discomfort and then do something about it.

10. Be mindful of the words you feed to others — you may have to eat them.

11. Communication and connection are the point.

Pink Post-It® Note

I have a pink Post-it note on my desk of a quote that I copied from somewhere a long while ago. It reads, "I am open to accepting all forms of abundance the universe has to offer me." I keep it for two reasons. One, as a reminder to myself to *allow*, to be receptive. The other, perhaps more important part for me, is the part about "all forms of abundance."

Opportunities can come from the most unlikely places, so long as you're willing to receive them. Hindsight is 20/20 and when you look back over a path, the way is far clearer than when you were busy moving forward. What, when looking backward, seems like a straight line, was actually a hop-scotch jump and skip in real time. A couple of years ago, I gave the keynote speech at a technology conference on the "Business of Communicating Joy." It was a rousing success and a terrific all-around experience, and the opportunity might never have found me if not for a series of events that began with a Facebook reconnection several years ago. Or, rather, I might not have found it.

We have the choice to choose to be aware, or not. We have the choice to be open to possibilities and pathways we hadn't started out on, or not. I believe that there is a richness of opportunities that constantly surround us. The question is, are you looking at/for them? Harvard Business Review published a great article on problem-solving and asking yourself the right question[16]. The article detailed how reframing the question and asking what "could" you do, as opposed to what "should" you do, can change everything. Reframing that one small question allows for a world of abundance to stand at your doorstep.

As an entrepreneur or a *maker*, I can't allow opportunities to remain unconsidered. It doesn't mean that I say "yes" to everything. Saying "no" and doing it well is an art form. What we're talking about is allowance. Being open to allow a deviation, a pivot, an innovation, or an unknown to affect our path is the idea. If we change our interior conversations from "what should I do?" to "what could I do?" the possibilities are abundant and epic.

Camera Skills (Virtual-Ready)

We know that being on camera can be scary. Unless you're a selfie diva, most people find something, or many things about themselves, with which to be self-conscious in everyday life. In our own heads, the camera magnifies our flaws. Who among us hasn't taken what we thought was going to be a great photo or video only to find that somehow slack-jawed ghoul has taken our spot?

No? Just me…?

A few years ago, my company was contacted by a super gigantic search engine technology company, (we're not naming names but you could

16 Gino, Francesca. "When Solving Problems, Think About What You Could Do, Not What You Should Do." Harvard Business Review. April 27, 2018.

GOOGLE it) to teach some of their people to appear more skilled and relatable on camera. In my many years of camera work as an actor and director, I've worked with all kinds of people — ranging from fearless hams to hunks of wood. The technology people were no different. Well, they asked a LOT more questions, and may have been more wood than ham, but they had the same fears and concerns we all do. The point is, that while Hollywood may be packed with skilled magicians, everyone can grab a little on-camera magic for themselves, if you know how.

Here are some important things to understand:

1. Yes, that is you. Get used to what you look like. Embrace the "flaws" and learn to work with them, around them and through them.

2. Every professional piece of content put out by Hollywood, advertisers and marketers has been touched, manipulated and massaged. Nobody wakes up like that. Nobody. Again, perfection is marketing.

3. Understand the light. Know where it is and where it's hitting you. It'll make the difference between looking like a Disney Princess and shoe gum.

4. Stop, STOP shooting videos while you're in your car. Whoever started that trend should be chained and jailed. Please just stop it. The entire universe thanks you.

5. Wear clothes that are neat, clean (yes, we have to say that), and are a flattering color on you. If someone asks you if you're unwell and you feel fine, that's a good indication that what you're wearing is NOT a good color. I personally can't wear yellow. Ever. It's terrifying.

6. SPEAK WELL. Yes, be yourself, be your best self. You can still enunciate and use all the good words.

7. Be confident. It transcends the lenses and creates a rapport and relationship with your audience.

8. During virtual meetings, please raise your computer camera several inches so you're not looking down on the lens, otherwise you'll look like a Shar-Pei puppy.

9. Talk to the camera as your audience, not something to be feared. Understand who your message is for and *have a conversation with them.*

Understanding these few things can go a long way to upping your on-camera skills. Don't forget to practice and invite trusted others to view your content for honest feedback. The key is not to get hung up on how we look, but rather to assure that the message we want to convey is being communicated in a professional and authentic way.

Going to the Show — My TEDx Dream

I'd been working for months on my TEDx talk. Actually, I've been working on it for years but maybe didn't know that I was working specifically for IT.

I knew the first time I applied (and I applied many times) that I had something to say. Something about communication and soft skills and how working in the theatre helped me... well, helped me everything. Each year I was rejected. But this last time was different. My friend Diana, who was familiar with the speaker vetting process, knew that they looked for personal, relatable stories. Not just people with a topic to lecture about.

Women. Women are important to me. Women like myself, my daughter and my mother and grandmother. All important to me and my *becoming*. So, for my topic, I submitted the idea that I had been talking about in some workshops and events — that we women can do a better job speaking about and for ourselves. Again, I've spoken on this subject for a couple of years to a variety of women-centric organizations.

In going through the selection process, the people who vet for TEDx kept asking me how my talk would be relevant to men in the audience. I wonder now if my talk had been about penis enhancement if they would have questioned how relevant it would have been to women...? I must have convinced them because in December 2018, I was notified that I had been chosen to be included in TEDx 2019. Holy crap!

When I saw the email, I opened it with a great deal of angst. I skimmed the first few words — enough to know that I had been chosen, and almost passed out. My heart raced and I was grinning like a fool. I think I was riding in the car with my husband when I read the email. I showed it to him and he began to grin like a fool too. Giving a TED talk had been a goal of mine for years and here it was — it was going to happen. Again, holy crap!

There was a small part of me that stepped back and said "you still have to actually give the talk, so don't go all bonkers yet." My interior voice is a realist. And a drag.

The speakers basically had three months to draft, polish and finalize their talks and slides. Speaker coaches were available to us to help us through the process, and you can bet your ass that I availed myself of their expertise. Sure, I'm a public speaker and sure I've probably given more talks to more people than most of the coaches combined, but this was TEDx and I wanted to be at the top of my game for this very particular type of presentation.

We were given photography and video appointments. TEDx is not a haphazard event and details were handled with precision. I met with my "personal" coach for the first time. He was an interesting, warm and funny person who was so supportive and caring throughout the process. No one could have asked for a better TEDx guide. The "kick-off" event was thrilling and a chance to meet many of the other speakers and performers, and it was one step closer to becoming real.

It's hard to believe or put into words, the *before*, when I'm sitting here typing after. I worked hard on my talk. And I didn't. I have a very particular set of skills that allow me to do this kind of thing better/easier than some people. So I spent the three months polishing and distilling and parsing my text, and less time on the how of delivery. I know how to use my voice, how to move, when to pause, etc. It was the text that made me a little skittish. In order for the talk to be as impactful as I wanted it to be, I had to be willing to share more of myself than I would normally and that scared me. I shied away from it and stopped working on my text for a couple of weeks.

We had a speaker rehearsal, and we were asked to simply tell a story from our talk or relevant to our talk. I told the Crisco story (you'll have to watch the talk to know exactly what I mean). It was scary for me to be that personally naked. Everyone in the room responded emotionally and I think that's what pushed me along. Knowing that people would respond and relate to a story about words.

I realized that months before I had booked a gig for what turned out to be, the night before the show. It was the day of the full dress runthrough for about 500 high school students and then I had to run to my booking. It was going to be a very, very long day.

I had planned to get to the theatre earlier than the students so I would have the opportunity to walk around on the stage, to live in the space. I ended up getting there late, and at that point, the theatre was open, there were people everywhere and the excitement was high.

I was the 2nd speaker to go on. Walking across the stage, smiling at Brian, the MC, I knew it was going to be good. I could feel the space around me filled with energy. Once I began, I felt the momentum begin to build. And when they responded to me, whether with small sounds or big laughs, I knew I had them — that they were with me. It was glorious.

I floated offstage to thunderous applause that day, feeling that I had done well and made myself proud. Backstage people hugged me and touched my shoulder, telling me that I had "crushed it." I practically glided upstairs to the balcony to watch the other speakers and performers. A couple of the coaches congratulated me as well as some other speakers who had watched. I was still floating in a pink euphoria.

During the first intermission, the woman who produced the event came to find me saying that a couple of people wanted to meet me. She took my hand and led me down the stairs to the stage, across it to the left and down into the audience. The students were milling around but as soon as a few saw me they ran over to me and told me how amazing my talk was. They told me how I had captured some of their awkwardness, and how empowered my words made them feel. They wanted to hug me and to touch me. I've never in my life felt anything like this. I was overcome with joy and surprise and love for all these young women. Women who were like me, that I was able to speak with directly. I felt uplifted and maybe, I felt grace.

It was a moment of perfection and I knew it within it. When I went back upstairs, I sat in a chair in the balcony and allowed it all to wash over me. Even now writing about it, my heart fills and I can't help but smile.

Later that day, after rehearsal, I was shopping along King Street before I had to head to my gig. I was in a store, speaking with a sales person telling her that I was looking for a skirt for the TEDx event the following day. She asked me what TEDx was, since she had never heard of it. I explained that it was a day of speakers, performers and ideas.

200

At that moment, two teenage girls politely interrupted us to tell me how they had seen me speak and how empowered I had made them feel. They asked if we could take a picture together and the sales person agreed to act as photographer. The young women thanked me again and went on their way. Extraordinary!

The day of the actual TEDx event dawned warm and sunny. I hadn't slept well the night before because I was so excited! I made sure that everyone in the house had what they needed, including instructions for the day, before I jumped into the car to head Downtown. As usual, I was running behind where I wanted to be. Actually, I was late. My call time was about 9 a.m. and I didn't get to the theatre until about 9:25 a.m. It was a stressful way to start the day AND I ended up parking on the street and feeding a meter.

Before I go on stage, I like to be quiet and alone with myself. So, in the middle of all the hustle and bustle backstage, I planted myself in a chair off to the side in the makeup room and breathed. I could hear the audience — it was big. More than double then at the rehearsal the day before. I felt my energy, my excitement rise, even as I worked on my breathing. Once I knew the speaker before me had reached his last slide, I moved to the curtain on stage right so I could hear Brian introduce me. Even hearing my name in this venue was magical.

I walked out smiling. It felt good. I reached the red dot and took a breath. I exhaled and began.

I can't recount the talk moment for moment because I can't remember it. I know that the audience leaned into me. I know that they felt for me. I heard them gasp and laugh. I heard their sounds of agreement. They applauded multiple times for things I said. I missed a slide and it didn't matter, because I shared with them what needed to be shared and kept going. I loved them and when I said, "thank you" at the end, the applause was thunderous. I walked off stage with a bigger smile than should be humanly possible.

Another moment of grace.

And I thought to myself that maybe I couldn't always talk to my teenage daughter, maybe she would not be able to hear me as her mom, but these other people were listening, and maybe someday she would hear me.

At about 11:15, I had to leave to put money in the meter that would get me through until lunch time. Walking to the car, there were a number of volunteers outside, many of whom congratulated me on a great talk. The BeeGees might have been playing in the background as I walked back to the venue.

At the lunch break, I connected with David, my husband. It was wonderful having him there. I felt very loved and supported. As he and I were chatting, people were constantly coming up and congratulating me and asking for pictures and shaking my hand or telling me how awesome they thought my talk was. It was surreal and amazing. At one point, I was in the bathroom stall and heard women talking about my talk.

As David and I walked to the lunch tent, we were constantly interrupted by well wishers and congratulators. As we were eating, people came to talk to me. The people at our table congratulated me. It is extraordinary to know that my words made an impact. David told me how proud he was of me and it meant so much to have my partner there with me, supporting and loving me and giving me all the space to shine.

At the end of the day, I connected with my friend, who had seen a version of this talk several times before. We walked to the tent and the same thing happened. People walking and then stopping to congratulate me and telling me what an amazing talk I gave. She and I sat and chatted as people came up to us. After we snacked on some delicious hand-made pretzels, we made ready to leave. I was filled up with people and emotion and experiences and was desperate for some space and quiet.

We walked to our cars and I got in and just sat for a moment, reveling in the quiet and the joy. I called David to let him know that I was on my way home. He told me that he had another piece of goodness to share with me. Turns out that he rode the elevator in the parking garage with two TEDx-ers who, when David asked them who their favorite speaker was, both unanimously said "LB Adams!" My God, that made me so happy!

The entire experience was the culmination of a big, fantastic, hairy goal and one of the great joys of my life.

LB Adams
Charleston, SC
March, 2021

Acknowledgements

Words of appreciation have to go out to a number of people, starting with Danielle Featherson, who poked and nudged and cute-baby'd me into a first draft. This book might not have made it without her.

I want to thank the friends and family who took the time to read that first draft and offer their loving and respectful criticism of what might have been a hot mess with potential. Gray Somerville, Pamala Cutler, Robert Houle, Julie Hussey, Jaime Morris, Janet Bates and Diana Saillant — thank you from the bottom of my heart.

To my husband David, who as my friend and cheerleader, helped me do another really big thing. I love walking the path with you.

Additional Learning

John Maxwell — Mr. Maxwell and company have created a wealth of books centered on leadership, including "Failing Forward" and "The 21 Irrefutable Laws of Leadership."

https://www.johnmaxwell.com

Tim Ferriss — Author of the seminal "The 4-Hour Workweek" and one of my favorites, "Tribe of Mentors," Mr. Ferriss offers a variety of business and lifestyle information and advice.

https://tim.blog

Dale Carnegie — Author and empire-builder, Mr. Carnegie wrote the immortal "How To Win Friends & Influence People."

https://www.dalecarnegie.com

Stephen Covey — The company FranklinCovey, provides a variety of business and personal leadership management study tracks. Mr. Covey wrote the globally ubiquitous "7 Habits of Highly Effective People."

https://www.franklincovey.com

Seth Godin — Mr. Godin's blog is one of the most popular in the world. He writes about business, specifically marketing and I can share that "Purple Cow" was a game changer for me and my business. Seriously. Read it.

https://sethgodin.com

Chrissy Teigen — Cooking, humor & a very unique perspective are on tap from Ms. Teigen. While Chrissy's cookbook, "Cravings" is not strictly professional development, you need food to live and humor is ALWAYS welcome.

https://cravingsbychrissyteigen.com

Glennon Doyle — While Glennon is not strictly a "professional development" author, I would dare anyone to say that "Untamed" doesn't offer practical, provocative life skills information. Because "...you're a goddamn cheetah."

https://momastery.com

Practical Dramatics — Communication, soft skills, humor and confidence. Home of the acclaimed video podcast, "Snack-Sized Business" and destination for all things LB Adams.

https://www.practicaldramatics.com

John Zinsser — Co-Founder of Pacifica Human Communications. TEDx speaker and expert in conflict negotiation and organizational ombuds programs.

http://pacificahumancommunications.com

Brené Brown — TED speaker, multi-national best-selling author and researcher on the subjects of shame, bravery and leadership. If you haven't seen her Netflix special, watch it!

https://brenebrown.com/

Tina Seelig — Professor, author and neuroscientist, Dr. Seelig has some fascinating perspectives on creativity and "catching luck."

http://www.tinaseelig.com

Notes & References

Chapter 1: What the Hell Are Soft Skills And Why the Heck Do I Need Them?

Half, Robert. June 9, 2016. "Are (a Lack of) Interpersonal Skills Hurting Your Team? *Robert Half Blog* https://www.roberthalf.com/blog/management-tips/are-a-lack-of-interpersonal-skills-hurting-your-team

Feffer, Mark. April 1, 2016. "HR's Hard Challenge: When Employees Lack Soft Skills" *SHRM*. https://www.shrm.org/hr today/news/hr-magazine/0416/pages/hrs-hard-challenge-when-employees-lack-soft-skills.aspx

SHRM. 2019. "2019 State of the Workplace: Exploring the Impact of the Skills Gap and Employment-Based Immigration." *SHRM*. https://www.shrm.org/about-shrm/Documents/SHRM%20State%20of%20Workplace_Bridging%20the%20Talent%20Gap.pdf

Hagan, Shelly. September 6, 2019. "More Robots Mean 120 Million Workers Need to be Retrained." *Bloomberg*. https://www.bloomberg.com/news/articles/2019-09-06/robots-displacing-jobs-means-120-million-workers-need-retraining

Agarwal, Anant. October 10, 2018. "Data Reveals Why the 'Soft' in 'Soft Skills' is a Major Misnomer." *Forbes*.

https://www.forbes.com/sites/anantagarwal/2018/10/02/data-reveals-why-the-soft-in-soft-skills-is-a-major-misnomer

Medland, Dina. March 30, 2015. "Quantifying the Value of 'Soft Skills.'" *Forbes*. https://www.forbes.com/sites/dinamedland/2015/03/30/quantifying-the-value-of-soft-skills

Chapter 2: Everything Is Communication

Mar, Ohn. September 1, 2008. "Proud is Proud, Sighted or Not, Researchers Find." *The New York Times*. https://www.nytimes.com/2008/09/02/health/02prid.html

Anderson, Stephen R. 2010, Update 2012. "How Many Languages Are There in the World?" *Linguistic Society of America*. https://www.linguisticsociety.org/content/how-many-languages-are-there-world

Strain, Kelly. March 30, 2020. "How Much of Communication Really is Nonverbal?" *PGi Blog*. https://www.pgi.com/blog/2020/03/how-much-of-communication-is-really-nonverbal/

Chapter 3: Hell Yes, The Words You Choose Matter!

Nordquist, Richard. July 17, 2019. "Biased Language Definition and Examples." *ThoughtCo*. http://thoughtco.com/what-is-biased-language-1689168.

McKean, Erin. 2014. "Go Ahead, Make Up New Words!" *TEDYouth*. https://www.ted.com/talks/erin_mckean_go_ahead_make_up_new_words?language=en

Lopez, German. February 2, 2016. "The Sneaky Language Today's Politicians Use to Get Away With Racism and Sexism." *Vox*. https://www.vox.com/2016/2/1/10889138/coded-language-thug-bossy

Heitler, Susan, PhD. March 9, 2015. "Should You Use This Word? It Decreases Your Effectiveness." *Psychology Today*. https://www.psychologytoday.com/us/blog/resolution-not-conflict/201503/should-you-use-word-it-decreases-your-effectiveness

Chapter 4: If Nothing Else, Read This Chapter On Public Speaking

Cuddy, Amy, PhD. 2012. "Your Body Language May Shape Who You Are." *TEDGlobal*. https://www.ted.com/talks/amy_cuddy_your_body_language_may_shape_who_you_are

Gilbert, Elizabeth. 2009. Eat, Pray, Love. New York. *Bloomsbury Paperbacks*.

Hollis, Rachel. 2018. *Girl, Wash Your Face: Stop Believing the Lies About Who You Are So You Can Become Who You Were Meant to Be*. Nashville. Thomas Nelson Incorporated.

Chapter 5: It's Time To Woman Up

Sandberg, Cheryl and Grant, Adams. January 12, 2015. "Speaking While Female." *The New York Times*. https://www.nytimes.com/2015/01/11/opinion/sunday/speaking-while-female.html?_r=0

Chapter 8: You Are Not For Everybody — Embracing Your Uniqueness

Chernow, Ron. 2004. *Alexander Hamilton*. USA. The Penguin Press, a Member of the Penguin Group (USA) Inc.

Miranda, Lin-Manuel. *Hamilton*. 2015. https://www.linmanuel.com

Chapter 9: Another Riff: Empathy And Why Everything Is Not Always About You

Merriam-Webster. "Empathy". *Merriam-Webster*. 2021. https://www.Merriam-Webster.com/dictionary/empathy

Streep, Peg. January 23, 2017. "6 Things You Need to Know About Empathy." *Psychology Today*. https://www.psychologytoday.com/us/blog/tech-support/201701/6-things-you-need-know-about-empathy

Krznaric, Roman. November 27, 2012. "Six Habits of Highly Empathetic People." *Greater Good Magazine: Science-Based Insights for a Meaningful Life*. https://greatergood.berkeley.edu/article/item/six_habits_of_highly_empathic_people1

Purse, Marcia (medically reviewed by Daniel B. Block, MD). June 15, 2020. "How Sociopaths Are Different From Psychopaths." Very Well Mind. https://www.verywellmind.com/what-is-a-sociopath-380184

Chapter 10: Squad Goals — Being A Stellar Part Of The Team

PBS.org. "The Great British Baking Show." 2010. PBS. https://www.pbs.org/show/great-british-baking-show/

Doer, John. "What Matters: Why OKRs?" https://www.whatmatters.com.

Chapter 11: Conflict Is Scary And *Mostly* Necessary

Kaplan, William. 2017. *Why Dissent Matters: Because Some People See Things the Rest of Us Miss.* Canada: McGill-Queen's University Press.

Joustra, Robert J. November 1, 2013. "The Tenth Man." *Capital Commentary* (A Publication of the Center for Public Justice). https://www.cpjustice.org/public/capital_commentary/article/264

Gallo, Amy. March 17, 2016. "How to Disagree with Someone More Powerful Than You." *Harvard Business Review.* https://hbr.org/2016/03/how-to-disagree-with-someone-more-powerful-than-you

Chapter 13: But Wait, There's More!

Idiart, Brook. July 25, 2017. "Why Kindness Matters In The Workplace." *Forbes.* https://www.forbes.com/sites/forbescommunicationscouncil/2017/07/25/why-kindness-matters-in-the-workplace/2/#60aefa01c72f

Gibbs, Adrienne. July 27, 2017. "Want to Improve the Workplace? New Research by Lady Gaga's Foundation Quantifies Kindness." *Forbes.* https://www.forbes.com/sites/adriennegibbs/2017/07/27/want-to-improve-the-workplace-new-survey-by-lady-gagas-foundation-quantifies-effects-of-kindness/?sh=644c6d2e6792

For more information about the author, her presentations and workshops, or to receive Practical Dramatics' e-zine, **Communiqué**, please visit www.practicaldramatics.com.

Connect with Practical Dramatics on social media:

 @practicaldramatics

 @thelbadams & @PracticalDramatics

Watch Snack-Sized Business:

 Practical Dramatics

Made in the USA
Columbia, SC
20 August 2021